ANDROPOV'S CUCKOO

A Story of Love, Intrigue and The KGB

by

Owen Jones

Copyright

Copyright © Owen Jones March 15th, 2025
Fuengirola, Spain.

Andropov's Cuckoo
A Story of Love, Intrigue and The KGB

Published by
Megan Publishing Services
https://meganpublishingservices.com

ISBN: 978-1-0683538-8-8

Cover by GetCovers

The right of Owen Jones to be identified as the author of this work has been asserted in accordance with sections 77 and 78 of the Copyright Designs and Patents Act 1988. The moral right of the author has been asserted.

In this work of fiction, the characters and events are either the product of the author's imagination or they are used entirely fictitiously. Some places may exist, but the events are completely fictitious.

All Rights Reserved

Dedication

This book is dedicated to my wife, Pranom Jones, for making my life as easy as she can – she does a great job of it.
Karma will repay everyone in just kind.

Inspirational Quotes

Believe not in anything simply because you have heard it,
Believe not in anything simply because it was spoken and rumoured by many,
Believe not in anything simply because it was found written in your religious texts,
Believe not in anything merely on the authority of teachers and elders,
Believe not in traditions because they have been handed down for generations,
But after observation and analysis, if anything agrees with reason and is conducive to the good and benefit of one and all, accept it and live up to it.
Gautama Buddha

Great Spirit, whose voice is on the wind, hear me.
Let me grow in strength and knowledge.
Make me ever behold the red and purple sunset.
May my hands respect the things you have given me.
Teach me the secrets hidden under every leaf and stone, as you have taught people for ages past.
Let me use my strength, not to be greater than my brother, but to fight my greatest enemy – myself.
Let me always come before you with clean hands and an open heart, that as my Earthly span fades like the sunset, my Spirit shall return to you without shame.
(Based on a traditional **Sioux** prayer)

"I do not seek to walk in the footsteps of the Wise People of old; I seek what they sought".
Matsuo Basho

"Have I not commanded you? Be strong and courageous. Do not be afraid; do not be discouraged, for the LORD your God will be with you wherever you go".
Joshua 1:9

"Whatever misfortune befalls you [people], it is because of what your own hands have done- God forgives much-"
Quran 42:30

Myself when young did eagerly frequent
Doctor and Saint, and heard great Argument
About it and about; but oft-times
Came out, by the same Door as in I went.
Omar Khayyam
The Rubaiyat XXIX.

Contents

ANDROPOV'S CUCKOO i
Copyright ii
Dedication iii
Inspirational Quotes iv
Contents vi
1 WILLIAM DAVIES 1
2 YUI MIZUKI 9
3 NATALIA PETROVNA MYRSKII 17
4 SUMMER 1967 27
5 YURI VLADIMIROVITCH ANDROPOV 35
6 OPERATION YOURIKO 47
7 THE PLAN IS AFOOT 57
8 THE KGB 67
9 THE DAILY GRIND 75
10 THE HOLIDAY 85
11 LUBYANKA 95
12 GULAG ARCHIPELAGO 105
13 A NEW JOB 115
14 LENINGRAD 1978 125
15 MUSHY-BRAINED AND DEWY-EYED 137
16 SOCHI, KRASNODARSKAYA KRAI 147
17 THE FULL BOTTLE 157
18 THE MULE TRAIN 167
19 THE LAST LEG 179
20 CHELTENHAM 191
21 EPILOGUE 203
22 AFTERWORD 205

DEAD CENTRE	207
About the Author	219
Review	221
Books by the Same Author	223

Andropov's Cuckoo

1 WILLIAM DAVIES

"He's coming back, Peter!"

"Hang on to him!" ordered the cardiovascular surgeon as he quickly scanned the machines and monitors on the racks above the opposite side of the bed with a well-practised eye. "Don't let him lose consciousness again, it might be the last time if we do."

All the flashing, spiking and streaming lights on all the monitors were normalising, as were the beeps and buzzing sounds.

"Come on, William, don't go to sleep on us now," he urged his patient.

"I'm trying not to," I heard myself saying in my head, but I couldn't get my lips to voice my thoughts. In fact, for a while, I thought that I had died ten minutes before I heard the first voice speak. The only reason I had for doubting my demise was that I'm a Spiritualist, and I have always believed that friends and relatives waited on the Other Side to welcome the dying over. There had been no-one waiting for me… Not that I have many friends or relatives dead or alive, although there was one I knew I could count on.

I had to put myself into the doctors' hands and trust in their ability. I wanted to give them a sign that I could hear them, so I tried to drum my fingers and wiggle my toes, but had no idea whether they were moving or not. I guessed not by the lack of reaction from the doctors and nurses who were obviously surrounding the bed trying to help me.

"His eyes are twitching, I think he's trying to open them," observed a female voice emotionally. Emboldened by such encouragement I tried harder, and, after a minute or so, I could see a kindly male face smiling down at me through a crack in my eyelids.

"Welcome back, William", he said seeming to mean it, "we thought we'd lost you that time. Welcome back to the land of the living. I'm terribly sorry about this, Old Man, but I have to rush off now that you're going to be all right, but these ladies and gentlemen are supremely competent and will take care of you just as well as I could. I'll see you later".

He whispered his instructions to the others and left.

It is strange, but when you have very little strength left, you can feel it ebbing or returning remarkably easily. In my case, I was getting stronger by the second. I don't know what drugs they've given me, but they and the will to live are working wonders.

"We'll keep you in tonight, William, but if the signs are good tomorrow, you can go back to your own bed. That'll be nice, won't it?"

I tried to nod and smile, but instead, I felt a tear run out of my left eye down over my temple and into my ear. I haven't slept in my own bed for nearly three years, but I knew what she meant of course. She was just trying to be kind… upbeat, and I did appreciate it. It's just that it's funny what you think about when you realise that you might be drawing your last breaths.

I don't consider myself religious, although I suppose others might. I believe simply in life after death, reincarnation and Karma. Therefore, death has never held any terrors for me, and life is only slightly preferable because it allows a wider range of experiences and more of them.

My last thoughts had not been about life or death or even meeting my Maker, they had been about the people I have loved, and especially the females, because I had always preferred theirs to male company. You could argue that that was my life flashing before my eyes, but it was a niche, edited version and it didn't flash. It lingered in a languid, lavish, seductive fashion.

In fact, I don't believe that that film of my life would have finished if I had died from the heart attack when I thought I might have. It would have carried on and I would have been without a body – the only change.

I have been a big, strong man all my adult life: over six feet and over sixteen stones, but fit and healthy with it. I have been ill and broken bones, but nothing has floored me for long. However, I fear that those days are at an end, because that was the second heart attack you just saw me recover from, and I am realistic enough to know, that I will probably not be able to ignore the third call to leave this Mortal Coil.

To be honest, I'm not all that sure that I would want to anyway. I am now seventy-one, living in an old people's home in southern Spain and my wife and friends have all gone on before me. Don't get me wrong, it is a very comfortable hospice, operated especially for English-speaking oldies like myself. It really is very nice, but it's not home, as I am sure you can appreciate and the bed they referred to as my 'own', is not the one I shared with my wife until she died two years, three months and seventeen days ago.

Actually, she was rushed from our bed into hospital and died there without recovering consciousness. She didn't survive her first heart attack. It's a shame, I thought she would have… when the time came. I slept in a hotel after that for a while and then I moved into the hospice – God's Waiting Room, we residents call it!

Anyway, I digress, but I'm afraid you will have to forgive me, dear reader, for it is true, an old man's mind does wander. However, if you have the tenacity to stick with me to the end, I will tell you the story of a woman that I want the whole world to know.

Trying to tell the story of someone else is difficult, and in this case it is obscured by the mists of time and an old man's power of recollection, but I will get there, I promise you that most sincerely

I am the eldest child in my family, of my generation in our family, I should say, three years older than my next sibling, so for a long time, I was like an only child. I was lucky though, because there were lots of children in the nearest five houses to ours and as luck would have it, eight of those nine children were girls. I loved them all in my preschool days as I had no sisters of my own… I have fond memories of playing Daddy to their Mummy at make-believe tea parties.

Most of them were years older than myself, so when they started school they found new friends and eventually, so did I. It was there that at the age of six I fell in love with a girl called Debbie. One day, after school, at the age of seven, we were sitting on the swings in the thunder, lightening and rain and hoped that a bolt of lightening would send us to a romantic death together. It didn't, of course, all it got us was a telling-off from our parents.

Then there was Sally when we were nine. I used to stalk her and when she said that I was the third most handsome boy she knew, I was in Seventh Heaven. At fifteen there was Lesley, whom I loved from afar, but never ever spoke to, and so it went on until I was seventeen.

I will never forget those wonderful girls, our innocence and the great times we had, or I wanted to have, together.

Some things you cannot tell, even at seventy-one and fresh off your death bed, and other things you don't want to tell because they are memories best savoured in private. I often wonder whether those early loves, for lovers they were not, remember me fondly too, but I will never know now and that is probably for the best. I can pretend that they do.

You see, I cannot ask them, because I have always moved around and never kept in touch. It is a reason for the lack of friends and close family. First, I went to university a hundred and fifty miles from home and then I joined the Diplomatic Service, which also involved travelling... but I am starting to get ahead of myself.

Between the ages of eighteen and twenty-three, the girls I was going out with started to become women, and that was even more exciting. I remember Janine, Glenys and Andrea... so many more friends and lovers alike. I dream about them all often, and in a way which is not disrespectful to my wife.

The nurse has come to put me to sleep... not like an old dog, you understand, more in the manner of a sick child, which I am frightened I am in danger of becoming. It is a reason for wanting to tell you my story soon. I will do my best to get on with it tomorrow.

∞

Muesli and fresh pineapple crowned with plain yoghurt for breakfast accompanied by a cup of weak herbal tea. I can't tell which one from the flavour, but it is all very nice, if predictable. I am not going to be in a fit state for jogging for a while, so I need plenty of roughage. The tea is probably a mild laxative as well.

Anyway, I have become aware over night, that, if my story is going to be published one day, it needs to be written down or recorded. A Dictaphone would be the least strenuous on me, so I asked the nurse who brought my breakfast to arrange for the hospice staff to buy me one. She tried to get out of doing it by reminding me that I would be 'going home' within eight hours, so I could ask them myself.

I wasn't having any of that though. 'I haven't forgotten I'm going back to the hospice today if I'm well enough!' I told her. 'Phone them to get me a Dictaphone as I asked, please!' She went off in a huff, but at my age we are allowed to be a bit crotchety from time to time, it's expected of us and one of the compensations for old age. You could call it a prize for surpassing the allotted three score years and ten.

When my plates are being cleared away by a different nurse, I ask about my Dictaphone again. Ten minutes later she phoned me back on my bedside phone to say that it was being taken care of. They are pretty obliging here, on the whole, and where I live too.

While we are waiting for them to take me 'home', where my Dictaphone should be waiting so that I can recount the story I have been promising you, I will fill in the time by telling you a little more about myself, but don't worry, I will keep it brief. I do not want to bore you and the real story is not about me anyway. This is not an ego trip, as the dear old Hippies used to say.

I loved the Seventies, but was too young to enjoy the Sixties.

I was born the eldest child in Cardiff, South Wales, the UK to an industrious working-class family. My father was a carpenter when he finished his National Service, but soon had his own construction firm and he and my mother soon had a family of five boys too. We all grew up fit, strong and happy. Our parents were Spiritualists, and Dad took us to Church with him every Friday night when he did his healing to give my mother a well-deserved 'night off'.

However, religion was never forced upon us. In fact, our schools were Church of Wales, cubs and scouts were Methodist and our closest aunty was Catholic. Religion was just not an issue in our family or neighbourhood. The first two things I can remember my mother saying are that she would die before she was forty-two and that I should become a diplomat. Both of which came true.

English was my mother language, but I learned Welsh from the age of six and then French, German, Latin, Dutch and Russian to fluency and a little Chinese and Spanish. The Diplomatic Service pays a bonus for every language you can speak, which was a big attraction for me. So was the promise of foreign travel, as I had travelled and studied abroad by the time I was fifteen. I was a confident traveller by eighteen.

I particularly liked to hitch-hike, but then all the young people did it back in those days and it was safer than it is now for some reason.

As a person, I tend to be a loner and a thinker, although I wouldn't claim to come to more sensible conclusions than anyone else. However, I do try to, and that was one of the reasons they employed me in the Diplomatic Service. I had a great life in the Service, and lots of fun... but there I go again hijacking this story, bending it towards me and my life... Oh, yes, I forgot... we're waiting for the Dictaphone before we can get onto the nitty-gritty, aren't we?

I apologise for that, but I am as impatient as you must be. Honestly!

The journey from the hospital to the hospice was only a few kilometres, so didn't take long in the large comfortable ambulance they provided. In fact, we left the hospital without warning at eleven a.m. and I was sitting in a large comfortable chair in the hospice grounds overlooking the beautiful marina in Marbella waiting for my lunch by noon.

Now, I realise that you have been waiting quite a while for me to get to the point of this book, I haven't forgotten, although I can't quite remember how long it's been exactly, so when the nurse brought me my lunch, I asked about the machine again. She used her mobile to ring the desk, and assured me that it would be delivered within the hour. I smiled, thanked her and tucked into my boiled fish and salad, followed by yoghurt and tea again.

I like that sort of food, but I have always been easy to please in culinary matters as long as I'm not asked to eat junk food. In earlier days, I favoured Indian and then Thai food, but that is all but denied me now, as is cheese, my clear all-time favourite. I have always had a passion for cheese, fresh, crispy bread and red wine or beer, which are also very rare treats these days.

The food and the hour have both disappeared now, but the only change to my circumstances is that I feel sleepy. It's the sea air probably. If they don't bring me my new toy soon, I'll be asleep again... dreaming about people from my youth, people perhaps long dead... Maybe, I should be as well, what useful purpose am I serving here? Eating and drinking and spending money, but to what end? Just to keep myself alive? No-one cares except the owners of the hospice, and that would soon stop if my money ran out, which it won't... The dear old British government will see to that until I pop my clogs.

In a way though, I am being held back from my inevitable journey through yet another death and rebirth. I just can't help thinking that my money would be better spent elsewhere. I'm drifting again, I sense it. I need to stay alive to tell you my story, which is not really my story because it is not about me, I know, I've told you that before, but I have known this story for most of my life. That's why I'm keeping myself alive, not just for the sake of it.

If the truth be known, I am anxious to continue on to the next leg of my journey and have been for two years, seven months and fourteen days. I miss her so much, I could cry every time I think of her, tough old bastard that I think that I am... pretend that I am. Eventually, everyone believes the image and lets you get on with it... not realising that that's the last thing you want them to do really. I'm just too scared to show my feelings, that's the truth... but then most men are.

Well, it's too late to change now... Maybe in the next life or the one after that. It's a good job that infinity is so long, it gives you plenty of time to correct your failings and weaknesses and, Lord knows, I need it.

I'm getting a sudden, unexpected memory of Ricky, a boy from university. He was from Battersea and affected a Cockney accent. He tried to act like the cock of the walk, but asked me to take him for an Indian curry one night because he'd never had one and wanted to impress a girl who said it was her favourite food. He got so drunk on red wine and beer that he fell face down in his Chicken Madras blowing bubbles! Ha, ha, ha... Good old days. A waiter and I cleaned him up and I took him home to his girlfriend, who had a houseful of nude photos of herself taken by her female flatmate.

I can't remember the flatmate's name, but she was Jewish and took me to bed that night with more red wine. I feel bad that I can't remember her name, but Maria or Marsha seems to fit the face I see in my head. Strange, I haven't thought about those three people for almost fifty years.

Excuse me, I must have drifted off. There is a note protruding from under my saucer: 'Your Dictaphone is at reception. Please ring and it will be brought out to you'. I am as happy for you as for myself, dear reader, because now I will be able to fulfil my promise and you will be able to assess whether what I have been saying is true or not. Just a moment, please, while I make a call.

"Here you are, William. I took the liberty of putting it on charge while you were asleep. Have fun with it", said the girl who delivered it.

"Yes, thank you, I will," I replied cheerily, but thought 'What a saucy mare!' Some of the younger ones treat us all as if we're senile. It drives me mad. It is true that some of us are totally doolally tap, but not all… not yet.

I played with the Nokia, turning it over in my hands looking for familiar features. It was a simple one, just what I wanted… could be voice-activated too. I was no stranger to modern technology, but another sudden thought came into my mind. I have written thousands of reports, but never written a biography. Read many, yes, but not written one. I can't think how to start. Really! This is most annoying. I, we, have been waiting for the recorder for twenty-four hours and now I still can't start!

I picked up my saucer to finish my tea, and a warm breeze blew the note down the lawn. I realise that the story I want to tell, her story, could not have taken place unless other events had happened first… Well, in that case, since you have indulged me thus far, I will push you a little further and take you back to the very beginning, as far as I am humanly able. The real beginning of this story is in yet another country, which found itself in very trying circumstances almost a decade before even I was born.

The woman I really want to tell you about went by many names, but she was born Natalya in Soviet Kazakhstan, although we will have to start in Japan with the Mizuki family. I have pieced their story together over the decades from various case notes which I was able to uncover in my professional life as a diplomat, and from things that I was told and overheard. So, with my fully-functioning, brand-new Dictaphone, I will now tell you about the first performers in our drama, Yui Mizuki and her family and hope that I don't receive that third curtain call before we get to the end.

2 YUI MIZUKI

Mr. Hiroto Mizuki was working in a reserved occupation in the Ministry of Finance as a middle-ranking official in Tokyo by day, and as part of the Home Defence by night. In 1944, when he was twenty-seven, he was in love with a colleague who worked down the corridor from his office and he vowed to make her his wife, if they survived the current American onslaught. Hiroto and his girlfriend, Suzume, were from a similar social class, both Shinto, both revered Emperor Hirohito as a god, and were both convinced that it was not possible for Japan to lose the war – the greatest war that Japan had ever waged.

The first signs that they might be wrong were the disappearance of young men from the streets of their beloved, ancient capital, Tokyo, and it's merciless fire-bombing by the Americans. On the night of March 9th, 1945, almost 700,000 incendiary bombs were dropped, killing 100,000 people, injuring 110,000 more and destroying forty percent of the city in the inferno which spread rapidly through the largely paper and bamboo buildings.

Suzume's faith started to crumble as her nerves shattered. After another bad night of bombing on July 20th, when a huge pumpkin bomb – a forerunner of the atomic bombs to come – was dropped near her parents' home where she also lived, she implored Hiroto to take her away. At a meeting in her home on July 21st, she could take it no longer, she told him on her bended knees. If he did not take her away very soon, she would either have to go alone or 'take the only other honourable way out'. Her parents gave them their blessing and a hurried Shinto wedding ceremony was arranged.

"But where can we go?" asked Hiroto. "I have no clear idea what is happening here in our own country, but I think that the south is safer – anywhere away from Tokyo, which they seem intent on bombing flat, along with everyone in it". Hiroto sipped his tea, pretending to be giving the matter his undivided consideration, in order to instil confidence into his terrified young fiancée. However, he hadn't a clue, he could see only one option.

"My father and mother have a comfortable farm in the south," he mused, "we could go there… They've hardly seen any fighting at all".

"That's fantastic!" replied Suzume beaming admiration at him. "Where is it, do tell us?"

"Well, if the trains were running, it is only about twelve hours away…" he said smiling, enjoying teasing his bride to be, "and if we had a car, and petrol of course, it is about nine hours away, but there are none of those things any longer… So, if you really want to go, it will take twelve to fourteen days to walk there. Do you still want to go?"

"With you by my side, my love, I don't care if it takes a month, but where is it?"

"Ten miles north of Hiroshima. It's beautiful and so quiet!" he replied. "We'll be safe there, and my parents will be happy for us to stay with them. Will you come with us, future mother- and father-in-law?"

The old man looked at his wife.

"No, son. You take care of our daughter and have many children. Our Fate, good or bad, lies with the Reigning Emperor and his capital. We will stay here. Anyway, we couldn't walk to Hiroshima even if we wanted to, it's much to arduous for us".

"We'll come to visit you after the war is over and the trains are running again", Suzume's mother comforted her.

They worked the following four days, and then called in sick to ensure that they would get another month's salary each and to give them time to sell Hiroto's unnecessary belongings, get married and take their leave of Suzume's family. Then, dressed as peasants in baggy clothes, with dishevelled hair and packs containing food concealed in a change of clothing, they set off to join the throng of refugees heading south for a quieter life on the morning of Friday July 27th.

Life on the road was hard, they had money concealed about their persons and food in their bags, but most others did not. They felt terribly heartless sitting away from the others, denying starving children food, because if they gave any away, they too would be begging soon. It would not have been so bad if there were shops along the way, but the movement of people along that grim and dusty road had been so heavy and so relentless for so long, that there was nothing left, and food was already scarce as it was because of the blockades and the bombing. All that could be seen as far as the eye could see were derelict farm houses and ravaged fields. There was no livestock, it had already been eaten, sold or hidden as future collateral. In it's own way, walking through the countryside was even as depressing as staying in Tokyo, except that the air was cleaner. Cleaner, but not sweeter.

One of the happiest moments of the day was ticking another twenty-four hours off, and the saddest moments were having to walk around the corpses of those who had died in their tracks. Often fights would break out for the deceased person's possessions, even his or her clothes and the body would be left naked to rot in the road, or it would be kicked into a ditch alongside it, if it smelled too bad. It was summer and hot, so it didn't take long for the flies and their baby maggots to start their gruesome work. They walked mostly at night because it was cooler, but that increased the risk of tripping over the rotting, dead bodies on the unlit roads. The smell of a putrid corpse was no warning as they were everywhere. They tried to keep reminding themselves that it was less than two weeks out of the rest of their lives together.

After eleven days on the road, they were near to Hiroshima.

"Come, Suzume, it's eight o'clock, let's have the last of our food. We can be at the farm in eight more hours. If we had a phone, we could tell Mum to expect us for tea. That would give her the shock of her life! Come on, let's see if we can see the city from here".

He helped her scramble up a small hillock by the roadside, and they sat down. She looked around to check whether anyone was watching before pulling a small parcel from under her clothing.

"We have a little rice from yesterday, my dear, and one last tin of fish. Can you see anything from over there?"

"No, not really... I'm not sure, the morning mist, you know? Come on, move over here, if the sun warms it up, it may clear soon and we may catch a glimpse".

Suzume moved over to the south side of the top of the mound and they sat down. Hiroto looked at his watch.

"Hmm, eight ten, Dad'll be shouting at the field hands now calling them lazy so-and-so's and Mum will be cooking and cleaning and scolding the maid for her slovenliness. Some things never change, do they, dear, despite all the mayhem, life still goes on?"

She emptied the fish out over the rice and put the cloth on the grass between them

"Tuck in," she said, "bon appétit..." as Hiroto took a tiny portion of fish and rice with his chopsticks, he heard his wife ask, "Look at that, Hiroto, whatever can it be? It's very frightening".

"What is it, my dear?" he asked looking up. His mouth dropped wide open as a huge cloud, the shape of a mushroom, but the size of a mountain grew before them. They instinctively hugged each other in fear just in time to miss the flash, but they could not escape the wind. First, the makeshift plate with it's small offering of food was blown away, and then the couple were blown over backwards down the north slope of the mound. They rolled down into the smelly, fetid water of the irrigation ditch at the bottom near the road, but it probably saved their lives.

As they tumbled down they caught glimpses of their fellow travellers being blown about and knocked down like skittles. They were the lucky ones, bits of broken wood, bamboo poles and even small rocks were being fired at those still standing as if from a blunderbuss. They didn't remain on their feet for long and all the time the wind sounded as if it were escaping from Hell itself, hot, fierce, strong and angry.

Then it was over... and an eerie silence reigned, for a moment, just long enough to pick up your head and wonder what had happened and look around at the devastation. Then the wind came back from where it had gone, but not all of it returned... it was less fierce, less hot and less angry, as if it were ashamed of the havoc it had wrought.

As the ringing in their ears eased, they could hear screams of pain and fear from people lying in the road or wandering along it aimless. Some were naked other were wearing rags. Many were wounded with poles or sticks poking out of them like Spanish bulls in a ring. Others were blind... many of them were blind, they were bumping into one another, falling into the ditches along the road and tripping over the bodies that were either too lifeless or too frightened to get up.

Suzume opened her eyes and screamed. She yanked her thumb from the thing she had been hanging on to for some kind of stability – the open mouth of a long-dead body. The corpses in the ditch had been revealed when the water was either blown away or evaporated, probably both. The other arm was around Hiroto, he scooped her up in his arms and took her to the top of the mound. Cautiously at first, but the tempest seemed to have passed. She was shivering, in danger going into shock, but there was nothing he could do except talk to her.

"Wha... wha... what kind of a Devil was that, Hiroto?" she stammered, her eyes as wide as saucers.

"I don't know, my dear. Perhaps a munitions factory exploded – sabotage, bombing or an accident. Don't worry about that now. Have a drink of water". He took a flask from inside his robe and held it to her lips as she was trying to clean imaginary bits of rotten flesh from her thumb on the grass.

"Did you see what I had my hand in?"

"Try not think about it, my dearest", he admonished tipping a few drops of water onto her thumb and drying it in his clothing. "Let's take a little rest, then we'll continue and get away from these sad, awful people".

In fact, those who could stand up were already wandering off in all directions except theirs, but some just walked until they fell and stayed put, crying like babies.

An hour later, the road was pretty clear of southbound travellers, and the traffic from the south was starting to increase. Most of those walking, which was not many, were in the same sorry state that they had already seen, but there were a few cars and buses, few of which were still trying to avoid the people in the road whether they were dead or alive.

"Stay here, Suzume, I must find out what happened. Take this", he said handing her his Home Defence Type 14, 8-shot Nambu semi-automatic pistol. I'll remain within sight, I just want to stop a car and ask what that cloud was".

"Please, don't be long, I don't like this place. The Kami are angry here and very powerful. Please hurry".

"I will my dear, don't worry, but I have to know... my parents... you understand?"

She did, and acknowledged that he had to leave her a while.

The vehicles heading north were not travelling quickly because of all the dead bodies on the road, some of which were badly mangled by the traffic with puddles of brains and intestines every few yards. However, nobody wanted to stop to talk to him either. Eventually, an army officer did stop and wound down his window, but held Hiroto at gun point.

He was a terrified young man, but he was not the officer he was pretending to be. He had an officer's pistol, a Nambu just like his own, and a lieutenant's cap on his head, but a private's uniform.

"Don't try anything", he ordered, "I'm not afraid to use this, you know?"

"No, I'm sure you're not. I won't come any closer. I am unarmed and mean you no harm. I just need to know what just happened. My parents live down there…"

"I doubt that they do any longer, sir. Nobody's alive down there… the whole of bloody Hiroshima has disappeared… there's just miles and miles of nothing… nothing at all, just ash and wisps of smoke and dead bodies… even more than this!" he said waving his pistol at the road. This is a bloody children's picnic compared to back there".

"What was it? Did a munitions factory or an ammo depot go up?"

"I don't know, I've never seen an exploding bomb make a cloud like that before or kill so many people. Whatever did that is fiendish, and so's the person who made it".

"Are you sure there's nothing left?"

"Nothing at all for twenty miles outside the city, sir, now I have to be going. Good luck, sir!"

"Wait… wait, can my wife and I come with you. We live in Tokyo… we can give you money when we arrive at my wife's parents' house… We were coming down to visit my own parents who live… lived just outside Hiroshima", he beckoned his wife to join him and she scrambled down the hill. "There doesn't seem much point in going on now and we've been walking for ten or eleven days. Here she is, it would be a great comfort to her, if we could ride some of the way with you".

"OK, hop in, but hurry I want to put all this as far behind me as quickly as I can. She's got a full tank, so she should get us most of the way, although I'm not sure where I'm going yet, just as far from this madhouse as I can get".

They got back to Tokyo on the 9th, just as it was announced that another, even larger atom bomb had been dropped on Nagasaki. Within a week

Emperor Hirohito had capitulated and the rape, pillage and plundering of Japan began in earnest.

The Mizukis moved in with Suzume's parents as Hiroto's place was no more and a homeless family had squatted the ground. He didn't have the heart to turn them away, when he had a real roof over his head. Then they returned to work on Monday 13th as if nothing had happened, but they only did that because of the money and the stability it gave them in their topsy-turvy lives. However, something had indeed changed and quite fundamentally so.

The Mizukis couldn't believe how stupid they had been to put so much blind faith in their so-called god-king, and they never wanted to see a war again. They found themselves drawn to the Communist Party of Japan as much by the phrases it used, like: 'Workers of the World Unite!' as by the horror and the disappointment Hirohito's folly had inflicted upon them, and the senseless atrocities that the American soldiers were committing every day.

Four years to the day after the end of the war in Japan, on August 14th, 1949, Suzume gave birth to a girl, whom they called Yui. They brought her up to behave like other Japanese girls, and her grandparents taught her Shinto, but her parents taught her Communist ethics, and showed her that the official explanation for events in the paper was never the only one, and often not even the correct one.

However, they kept all that 'non-traditional' Japanese side of their life secret, because the Mizukis had learned to trust no-one but their local Communist Party leaders. Life was very different in those early years after the war as the Mizuki family's fortunes changed with MacArthur's whims, though the CPJ looked after it's own with donations from Mother Russia and the Mizukis held good jobs. They were doing far better than most.

They rewarded their political benefactors with snippets of information, which were sent back to Moscow.

In 1967, Yui was accepted into Tokyo university to study languages – English, Russian and Chinese – her favourite subjects and her father put her name down for a job at the Ministry. They had three years to amass enough money to pay the necessary bribe for the job, but they were not concerned about that. They only wanted her to be able to move to the Foreign Office with an option to sit the examinations for the Diplomatic Service.

Yui's future was guaranteed, as long as she passed her finals at university. She never revealed her communist leanings, not to anyone ever. Her parents had instilled their own caution into her, and she had seen the wisdom of their strategy. Nevertheless, she attended some CPJ meetings as a member of the public and sometimes played Devil's Advocate by asking awkward, predetermined questions of the leaders on the podium.

However, some of the higher members of the CPJ did know who she was and her parents continued to play an active, but secret rôle. Despite her privileged position, all that Yui really longed for was the day when she could take up a job, earn some really decent money to help her parents in any way they wanted, and get out of Japan to escape it's stuffy traditions and old-fashioned ideas. She was a modern woman with ideas to match, so she felt stifled in her own country.

She had no real preferences, but the UK, Canada or the USA, would do for a start. Her upbringing and philosophy made her hate the rich elite of those countries as much as she hated those of her own, but also as a communist, she didn't blame the ordinary working classes who lived there.

She had no idea how she could achieve that goal and still honour her parents, but joining the Ministry of Finance, switching to the Foreign Office and then applying for a position in the Diplomatic Service, was the nearest that she had been able to come up with so far, and what was more, her parents were willing to help her achieve her ambition.

Yui buckled down and took one hurdle at a time, but she was not happy.

3 NATALIA PETROVNA MYRSKII

During the Great Patriotic War of 1941 to 1945, when the main objective of the Soviet government was the repulsion of the German invasion on it's western frontiers, Pyotr Ilich Myrskii was fighting the Japanese in Manchuria. This battle culminated in the defeat of the Japanese forces in the Soviet-Japanese War of 1945, which helped terminate World War II globally. He had little time off, but he did get home to Alma Ata, the then capital of the Kazakh Soviet Socialist Republic, to see his childhood sweetheart, Marina Antonova, once a year. Marina had had to curtail her degree in Japanese at the local university for the duration of the war to work in a munitions factory and she was also giving talks on Political Education to workers, locals, immigrants and migrants, at local factories, and to children at their schools.

Times were hard during the war and food was scarce, despite the number of farmers in the area, although Alma Ata and the province saw no war damage. The problems stemmed from a huge increase in the population. Many European Soviet citizens and much of Russia's industry were relocated to Kazakhstan during the war, when Nazi armies threatened to capture all the European industrial centres of the western Soviet Union. Large groups of Crimean Tatars, Germans and Muslims from the North Caucasus region were deported to Kazakhstan, because it was feared that they would collaborate with the enemy, and about a million Poles from Eastern Poland, which was invaded by the Soviet Union in 1939, were deported to Kazakhstan. It is estimated that about half of them died there. However, the local people became famous for sharing their meagre food rations with the starving strangers and more than 52,000 residents of the city received the title 'Gratitude for Your Self-Denying Labour'. Not only that, but forty-eight residents were granted the title of 'Hero of The Soviet Union'.

When he was demobilised in 1945, Pyotr returned to his job at a local engineering company, but he had an idea to better himself by learning technical drawing at night school. He wanted to design widgets rather than make them. Meanwhile, Marina went back to university and they both resumed their courtship. One starry evening, they made a commitment to one another to get married when they had passed their final exams.

As a member of the Communist Party and a political activist, Marina often regaled Pyotr for his bourgeois desire to 'improve himself', because it implied that designing was superior to manufacturing which, she said, created class distinctions and strengthened divisions in society, for such was the Party line, although in private she supported his ambition. She had to play the Stalinist Game though, because everyone knew they were living in dangerous times. Everyone remembered the Great Purge just before the war when at least a million people had been executed and perhaps five million were 'relocated', many to the network of Gulags or forced labour camps.

Marina was a realist, she knew that these things happened, but she didn't want them to happen to her, so she toed the Party line even with regard to her family and boyfriend.

One fine August weekday in 1948, after receiving notification that they had both passed their finals, they went down to the Registry Office in the city centre and tied the knot. Within a year, almost to the day, on August 14th they were blessed with a daughter, or at least they would have expressed it like that, if high-fliers in Soviet society had been allowed to believe in a God who could bless them.

Natalya Petrovna Myrskii was born, but even before she was twenty-four hours old, she was Natasha to her mother and Tasha to her father.

Marina was ambitious, cautious and faithful to the Party and she enjoyed the privileges that Party membership and her degree brought. In return, nothing was too much work for her, as long as it was the Party that asked her to do it. Consequently, Pyotr spent many nights playing with Tasha in front of the radio, while his wife was out with the activists spreading the latest words of Papa Stalin or Comrade Khrushchev, 'The Father of The Thaw'.

At first he felt uncomfortable about accepting the privileges that Marina's rank bestowed upon them, but as his own status in the firm rose, he too was granted extra food, extra drink and invitations to lavish dinners at the company's expense, to which he could take his wife. He was receiving about six such invitations a year and Marina about twice that, but at least he felt as if he was paying some of his way. On such occasions and when they were working, the grandparents took it in turns to look after Natasha for the first five years, but when she was old enough, she was enrolled in Infants' School – the best one the city had to offer, courtesy of the Party.

'That was to be expected', Marina assured Pyotr when he expressed doubts, 'all the children of prominent Party officials attended the best schools, so that their parents could concentrate on their jobs without having to worry about their offsprings' education'. Pyotr reluctantly accepted Marina's excuse because he wanted the best for his daughter, but in private he still wondered how having the best food and drink helped Party officials do their jobs any better. He often thought of broaching the subject with Marina, but knew that she would have an answer.

She always had an answer for everything.

In truth, he didn't like to get on the wrong side of her, because he was a little frightened of her. He feared her ambition and her determination, which was first to be elected as Ward Party Delegate, then as Chairperson of the Alma Ata Communist Party, then the Kazakh Republic and finally to become part of the Party Congress – the highest organ of government in the USSR.

She would admit so much to Pyotr, though not to anyone else, but what she could not even tell him was her dream to sit on the Central Committee and even become the first female member of the Politburo, following in the footsteps of her heroine and rôle model Elena Stasova, who had made it to the Central Committee in 1917 and 1918, but that was a lofty goal indeed.

Even Marina had to sit down went she dreamed of achieving that goal. It made her giddy to think about it, but she dared to dream that it was all possible in fifteen to twenty years. Perhaps thirty for the Politburo, but she was still only twenty-three, she had time on her side and lots of work to do first. Pyotr would have been really terrified of his wife, if he had known she harboured those dreams.

Natasha grew into a beautiful, well-educated, well-mannered teenager, although it is fair to say that she was being indoctrinated by her mother and the special schools she was studying at. She and the other pupils had to swear allegiance to the Soviet Union of Socialist Republics, salute the flag and sing patriotic songs and old battle hymns every morning before class, but it was actually no more than happened in the state and church schools of a lot of other countries in the West and the East.

They were trained to analyse current and past events in the light of the historical struggle of class, but they were not shown the weaknesses of their own political system. However, Natasha didn't know that. She was good at learning and enjoyed the praise of her parents and teachers for doing well. She regularly came top of her class, and showed an exceptional aptitude for languages like her mother, who had been teaching her Japanese since she had spoken her first word. At seven years of age, Natasha's Japanese was almost as good as her Russian and her native tongue, Kazakh, so her mother hired a private tutor to teach the family English. Natasha took to it like a duck to water, as she seemed to do with any lessons presented to her. However, Pyotr was less keen, and soon left the two high-fliers to their studies 'lest he held them back'.

That was his excuse anyway.

By ten years of age, Natasha was fluent in four languages and reading books in them too. She could also speak Polish reasonably well. This did not go unnoticed in a school that was looking out for the best students in order to showcase them to the world as examples of a socialist education. Natasha was started in classes on Latin, French and German, the idea being that Latin and French would give her an excellent grounding to all southern European languages and Latin, English and German would open the door to the northern ones. Similarly, Russian would be her entry point into the languages of the Soviet Bloc.

This already-proven strategy worked again and Natasha was soon using her swift mind and common-sense to predict words in languages she was studying even if she had never come across them before. She could see patterns in words and languages as easily as other people could see colours that matched or clashed. None of her teachers had ever come across such a gifted child linguist before.

By fourteen, her French, German and Latin was as good as any of the local high school teachers could take her, so she started sitting in on classes at the university. She had noticed the similarity between Latin, French, Italian and Spanish before, but she had not been in a position to do anything about it, however, now she had access to the university library and its brand-new language laboratory, so she took out a 'Teach Yourself' course in Spanish, because she had been learning about the Spanish Civil War in school.

She had a sense of humour as well, and loved to mimic the accents and mannerisms of famous people. The only two that were off bounds were Stalin and Khrushchev, her mother would not allow her to make fun of them in any way whatsoever, but her father enjoyed her performances when Marina was not at home, which was quite often, because as well as her Party commitments, she was Kazakhstan's foremost expert on Soviet-Japanese affairs, so she was encouraged and paid to spend periods over there. Sometimes, it was for a few days, sometimes a couple of weeks.

They were always disguised as 'cultural delegations' but they performed a multitude of tasks including giving pep-talks to the CPJ and bringing them special messages from Papa Stalin or Khrushchev to judging the mood of the people. The CPJ was undergoing a huge growth in membership during this period, partly in reaction to the prolonged American presence and partly because the Americans encouraged it as a counterbalance to civil unrest. She addressed massive rallies in Tokyo and other big cities in their own language.

After one such trip in 1963, she suggested to the Alma Ata Communist Party that they invite a group of Japan's most vibrant Communist Party activists to come to stay in Alma Ata for a week's paid holiday. The idea was cautiously liked and sent up the chain of command, from where it came back down again. It was approved by Khrushchev himself and rubber-stamped by the Politburo. Marina photographed the letter for her box of memorabilia and had the original framed and hung on the wall in the Alma Ata Communist Party Central Offices. She felt as if she were being noticed, and that she was another rung up her ladder, although another woman, Yekaterina Furtseva, had beaten her to becoming the first female member of the Politburo in 1957. Marina, studied, emulated and supported Furtseva's every move.

Funds were made available from Moscow and travel arrangements concluded, although they were not so straightforward. Marina was dispatched to Japan to deliver the good news, the arrangements and the funds.

"It's like this", she explained to the hierarchy of the CPJ, "we, that is Comrade Khrushchev and the Politburo, do not trust the Americans. They say they are happy to see the CPJ flourish, but they may just be trying to lull you and us into a false sense of security, so that they can find out more about us and our members. Therefore, comrades, it is imperative to maintain the highest levels of security and secrecy at all times.

"I have been authorised to advise you to select your ten delegates to our 'conference' in Alma Ata with the utmost care. They may bring their spouses, but the spouses will have to be vetted just as rigorously. Do you understand me, comrades? With the utmost rigour! We do not want to jeopardise the future of the honourable CPJ and its vanguard of brave comrades for the sake of a week's conference, which I might add will not be quite so rigorous, if you get my drift.

"Therefore, Comrade Khrushchev has recommended that you make a block booking at this hotel in South Korea and fly there at different times on different flights. You will fly into Seoul, and take taxis to the hotel, which is closer to the border. Your contingent should be assembled by the second Sunday in August. The owner of the hotel is sympathetic to our cause and will arrange for your safe passage into north Korea, from where we will fly you to Alma Ata without receiving entry stamps from either North Korea or the USSR.

After the week is up, we will reverse the procedure, and the hotelier will cover for you if necessary while you are away, but we are not anticipating any trouble, we have used this route many times before. When you arrive back in Japan, no-one will be any the wiser that you have not done exactly as you said you would.

"Last, but not least, here is a bearer bond drawn on an American bank to cover all your expenses".

"This is most generous of you, Comrade Marina Antonova, I… er we, don't know how to thank you, Comrade Khrushchev and the great people of the USSR for this honour and your generosity. You can rely on us".

It worked like clockwork and became a regular, annual event. Marina played host to the CPJ delegation and students of the Japanese language at the university acted as guides and mini-hosts and hostesses to the visitors. They laid on political lectures in the mornings, sightseeing trips or cultural events in the afternoons and dinner and more cultural events in the evening. The visits were a great success and earned the Communist Party of the Soviet Union and Marina Antonova herself many brownie points.

Marina could feel her goal getting closer, but it was still so far away. However, the 'cultural swaps' were not like working. She enjoyed playing Mrs. Bountiful to their Japanese comrades who were still living under fairly austere conditions in their own country, not that the Soviet Union was as well off as she was presenting it. She had to pick and choose her destinations quite carefully and even the routes to get there, since they didn't want the visitors to see the rows upon rows of dreary concrete apartment blocks that had been built for migrants in the city's suburbs, or the shanty farms that many of the peasant-like farmers still occupied.

One year, on one of these visits, she met a couple that she felt a particular affinity for, a Comrade Hiroto and his wife Comrade Suzume. She had read in their dossiers that they sometimes passed over snippets of information which were useful in a minor way, and she had been told to cultivate them with a view to getting higher grade information from them, but she found that she genuinely liked them anyway, which she found made her job easier.

Several times during their visit, when the evening's entertainment was concluded, she would invite them on to more restricted venues where they could continue eating and drinking the night away. Unfortunately, Pyotr did not speak Japanese and the Mizukis did not speak Russian, although they did speak some English, but Pyotr had given that up before he had learned anything, so she didn't bother to invite him.

Marina thought that he could be a bit of a bore at social events anyway, so only dragged him along when it was expected that her spouse should show an interest in her career. Pyotr didn't mind at all, it suited him just fine.

Natasha sometimes took part in the cultural events. For example, she would sing in the choir or perform traditional dances in the university troupe, but in general it was deemed that she didn't have time to indulge in such frivolous activities as cultural exchanges. Not that they were beneath her, her mother said, but she had to study, because they had other objectives planned for her, although no-one yet knew what they were precisely. Still, anyone who knew children knew that she was special and that her language skills were just phenomenal.

For their part, the Mizukis liked Marina, they respected her aura of power, although they thought that 'she could lighten up a little'. She always seemed to be scheming or plotting or looking for schemes and plots. Like a presidential bodyguard is always 'elsewhere' in his mind, Marina always seemed to be only half-listening. What they didn't realise was that in Russian society in those days, you only needed to maintain eye contact with the person you were talking to if you didn't trust them. If you did trust them, you were free to look around to see if anyone else was trying to listen into your conversation. You only stared into the eyes of those you didn't trust in Soviet society, the purges had taught everyone that lesson.

The Mizukis went on the 'August Kazakh trip' every year after their first. The CPJ couldn't always fund them, and then they would pay for themselves, but Marina always tried to put a good word in for them and always made a fuss of them. Likewise, when Marina visited Tokyo, they usually went out for dinner at least once or met at Suzume's parents' for a home-cooked meal. They had their own house by the mid-fifties, but even by the time that their friendship with Marina was flourishing, they were frightened of being spotted out with her in case they were under suspicion and being watched by American spies, although to the casual observer, Marina could pass for Japanese, or Korean, or half Japanese- half Korean and she always spoke flawless Japanese in Japan. She even dressed like a local middle-class woman.

This was not coincidence, many people from Alma Ata could pass for members of other nationalities, both Asian and European. It was a very cosmopolitan city and had been for centuries. The first people to settle there had done so during the Bronze Age in about 1000 BC, and from 1000 AD, it had been an important trading, craft and agricultural centre on the Silk Road and had even boasted it's own mint. It had been a melting pot of trading nations for centuries.

In fact, Marina's names were not the ones she was born with and neither were Pyotr's, who was also Asian in appearance. Their parents', like so many others, had taken the precaution of Russifying their names by deed pole in order to better blend in with the tens of thousands of real Russians who were being sent to Kazakhstan to colonise it, or help it, as they put it.

The state was building about 300,000 square metres of dwellings a year, and most of them made during this time were earthquake-proof blocks of apartments for non-Kazakhs. One consequence of Khrushchev's 'Virgin Lands Campaign', for that was how it was referred to in the press, was that by

1970, Kazakhstan was the only Soviet Republic in which the indigenous population was in a minority.

Many families had seen the writing on the wall and given up their original Kazakh names. That had been bad enough for many, but giving up the language and culture was another thing completely, except for Marina and others like her.

It was another aspect of Marina that Pyotr found rather unsettling.

ropov's Cuckoo

4 SUMMER 1967

As a special eighteenth birthday treat, Hiroto and Suzume invited Yui to go on holiday with them before she went to university in September. She jumped at the chance to go abroad for the first time in her life.

"Where will you be going?" she asked, "South Korea again?"

Neither she nor the Mizukis' non-CPJ friends knew that their true destination had been the USSR. Yui was thrilled to discover that they were actually going to the Soviet Union, where she could practice her Russian. She had often wondered why her parents kept going back to the same hotel in South Korea – it had seemed such a boring thing to do. This, however, was extremely exciting.

"We cannot impress on you enough though, Yui, that you cannot tell anyone about Alma Ata. Just say that we are going to South Korea again".

"I understand, Daddy. I won't say anything. You can rely on me".

"We know we can, darling", said Suzume, "that's why we want to take you with us this time. You are older now and more in control of yourself. We hope that you will find it a rewarding experience, as well as a fine holiday".

They had checked their plans with Marina first, naturally, and she had presented the suggestion to her committee, but everyone had thought it a fantastic idea, not least because it gave them the chance of another convert to the cause, another potential university graduate asset, which the Central Committee had recommended that all cadres try to cultivate. Graduate students got good jobs and having an asset in a good job in a foreign country meant infiltrating that country's power base, whether it be governmental or commercial. Both sectors had secrets that the Motherland could use in the struggle for International Socialism.

1967 was one of the years when the Mizukis had to pay for themselves, but they hadn't expected the CPJ to pay for their daughter and it was still a cheap holiday anyway, because they only had to pay for the return flights to Seoul.

Marina met the party at the military airport in North Korea and flew back to Alma Ata with them, where there was a coach waiting to transport them on to their hotel. Yui found the whole business terribly exciting. In fact, she said that just being in Tokyo airport waiting for their flight was the most exciting thing she had ever experienced. Then she said the same about the flight, and the same about the taxi journey to the hotel and the same about actually having her own room in the hotel.

The exhilaration she felt when being smuggled over the border into North Korea was almost too much for her to bear, as was being treated like a VIP in a foreign country and the USSR of all places! Seeing the prolonged vision of joy on their daughter's face made Hiroto and Suzume wish they had taken her with them before. As for Yui, she felt that the fifteen years of dreaming of living abroad had been justified. She was more determined than ever to leave Japan, but she didn't think it prudent to tell her parents that just yet.

When they had all checked into their Kazakh hotel, Marina took Suzume's hand, and said, one proud mother to another, "I have seen photos of Yui over the years, but they haven't done her justice. She is a very beautiful girl and not unlike my own daughter". She looked at her watch. "She's helping out at a local crèche at the moment, but I'll bring her with me this evening. I'm sure our daughters will become the best of friends. I'll see you at seven, I have to dash, bye-bye for now".

Natasha was looking forward to meeting her first foreigner, but Pyotr was rather less keen to have to go. He knew that one of the main slogans of the CPSU was 'Workers of the World Unite!" and he did agree with that sentiment, but he had fought against the Japanese in Manchuria and many of his friends and comrades had been killed, some horrifically, as in any war and he didn't want to let them down by fraternising with the former enemy. However, he realised the significance of his daughter meeting a new friend and so went to support her.

"It's going to be pretty boring for me though, Marina, isn't it? I mean, we don't have a language in common, do we?"

"No, Pyotr, but don't worry, if you can think of anything interesting enough to say, your daughter or I will translate it for you". She was trying to be funny, but the joke only hurt, making him feel even less like going.

"It's all right, Dad, I'll translate for you and just think, you'll have four beautiful women to look at while Mum and I have only got two old men".

That attempt at humour did make him smile, so he pulled his best jacket on and followed them downstairs to the taxi that would be waiting for Marina as a privilege. At least the first night would not be too rigorous, he thought, because of all the travelling the visitors had endured, surely, they would want to get to bed early. The venue was a top restaurant in the city, which had been reserved by the Party for the evening. There was to be a formal four-course dinner and traditional music played by two groups, one Russian and one Kazakh.

Marina, her family, the twenty-three visitors and two top Party officials and their wives were seated at a long top table. Marina sat in the centre with her family to her right and the CPAA officials to her left. The Mizukis sat opposite them. Marina's first job was to introduce her superiors to the visitors one by one, so she led them around the table and made the introductions.

Marina kept her welcome speech short because she had to give it first in Japanese and then in Russian for the sake of the one hundred-odd Party members seated at theirs and other tables in the room who didn't speak a word of Japanese. A brief reply thanking their hosts was given by the CPJ chairman and a few other Russian officials said something, none of which was not translated. When the formalities were over, the meal began and people started to relax.

Hiroto surprised the Myrskiis by leaning over and speaking to Pyotr in halting Russian. Pyotr found it difficult to understand because of Hiroto's heavy accent, but he tried and appreciated the effort Hiroto had made, and as the wine and vodka went down, he got used to the growling voice and communication got easier. Marina helped out more than she had suggested she would but less than she had expected to have to, mostly because the Mizukis had been studying Russian for the last twelve months without telling her, preferring to surprise her on their next visit.

The girls started by looking at each other and smiling quizzically at the awkward antics of their parents.

"Which languages do you speak, Yui?" asked Natasha.

"Russian, Japanese and English, any of them suits me fine, Natalya, whichever you like."

They flitted between Japanese and Russian easily, throwing in a few English words here and there when it seemed stylish or appropriate to get a particular nuance across.

"You speak English with an American accent," remarked Natasha.

"Yes, there are a lot of American soldiers and tourists in Japan and English-language television is nearly all American".

"I have an English accent. We try to speak the way they do on the BBC World Service in my school, but it is difficult because we're not supposed to listen to it at home. Our lecturers record programmes that are suitable and edit them, then they give them to us to practice with".

"A kind of censorship, you mean? Do you have censorship here?"

"I suppose I do, but it is for our own good. The organs of the capitalist governments of the West are masters at propaganda, and they would entrap the gullible. Young minds, such as students', are easily led, so they have to be protected. Don't you agree?"

"My parents tell me not to believe everything I hear in the American and Japanese media as well, because they say that the Americans control what is said".

"Yes, and I think that they are right too, Yui. You're lucky that you have intelligent and caring parents who can protect you from the lies. Your parents and all Japanese have close contact with the Imperialists, so they are well placed to advise their children, but Soviet parents have not had that contact, so here, the state does that for us, but the result is roughly the same, or do you not follow the wishes of your parents?"

"Oh, I listen. I take everything I see or read with a spoonful of salt, don't you worry…"

"Isn't the expression 'a pinch of salt'?" asked Natasha with a wry smile.

"Not where I live, Natalya, not where I live!" and they both started to laugh. Their mothers looked at their girls laughing behind their hands in the Oriental way and smiled at one another, pleased that they were getting along so well, so quickly.

The two families conversed easily for the rest of the evening and it was soon time to go their separate ways. The two girls hugged in the Russian custom, which felt strange, but nice to Yui and then bowed slightly after the Japanese tradition, which Natasha had learned at school.

When they arrived home, Natasha asked her mother what she had not dared to do in public. "May Yui sleep here in my room sometimes, Mum?"

"Certainly, I don't see why not, if her parents agree".

So, for the next six days and nights the girls were inseparable, sleeping three nights in Natasha's room and three in Yui's. On the first morning Natasha woke up in the hotel, she was very impressed by the amount of make-up that Yui and her mother had.

"This is so much better quality make-up than we have, Yui, and the range! How do you make up your mind, which one to put on? I envy you. I'm afraid we don't have these brands here".

Yui felt awkward so she just said, "Tash", she had picked it up from Natalya's father and liked it, "have you noticed how much alike we look?"

"Yes, I have. The major differences like hair, accent and posture could be dealt with, and with all this make-up we could easily hide our minor facial differences as well".

"Shall we have some fun, Tash? We could impersonate one another and see whether our parents can tell us apart! What do you say?"

"Oh, I don't know… I'm not cutting my hair like yours, sorry. No offence, but I like my long hair… it's taken me eighteen years to get it like this. Why do Japanese girls cut their hair, Yui?".

"No, you're right, it is beautiful. I had to cut mine for school, but I'm going to start growing it when I start uni next month… I know, we could wear hats! Is there a store near here where we can buy some cheap hats or caps?"

"Sure! Alma Ata is famous for cheap hats", she joked. So, they had their breakfast, dodged the organised trip to a war memorial that they hadn't wanted to go on anyway and went shopping. They returned several hours later with bags of gear, but one thing had struck Yui and that was the lack of choice, as Natasha had said, although it was far worse than she had expected.

She had been dismayed by the bleak make-up counter in even the largest department store in such a big city. They had dark-red lipstick and light-red lipstick but it was really unpleasant, having tasted oily and smelled of fish. Then there was the nail varnish, they had pink or clear, but nothing else and

Natasha had remarked how it wasn't always possible to buy the clear variety 'because the government had to prioritise the use of scarce resources'. The choice in the normal, local shops was even worse.

It hadn't been much better in the valuta shops – the special shops that only traded using foreign currency, which it was illegal for Russians to hold. It had been the same with clothing.

"There are shortages again", Natasha had explained apologetically, but Yui knew there and then that she didn't want to live in a socialist or communist country. However, she was polite, sensible and sensitive enough not to express her opinions, even to her new best friend.

They spent all afternoon laughing a lot, dressing up and making themselves up into a hybrid of them both. When Mr. and Mrs. Mizuki came back from their trip, first they saw Natasha watching television in her disguise. 'Hello, she had said in her best imitation of Yui's accent, but without turning around.

"New clothes, dear? And new make-up! You look very nice, Yui!" said her mother taking off her coat and hanging it up. "Doesn't she father?"

Hiroto was just about to agree, when Yui came out of her bedroom.

"Doesn't she what, Mum?"

At that point, Natasha had turned around and smiled and both parents had to do a double take, their mouths open in astonishment.

"Why that is just incredible! You two look like identical twins!" the girls moved close together, put their arms around each other's shoulder and pulled the same smile they had practised earlier in the dressing table mirror. Then they all started laughing.

"I couldn't, can't tell you apart. Even now that I know it… it's uncanny. Perhaps I need stronger glasses", said Hiroto, taking his spectacles off and staring at them, but it made no difference.

Natasha took off her imitation Carnaby-Street floppy cap and let her hair tumble down.

"Is that easier for you, Mr. Mizuki?"

"It could be a wig", he joked smiling.

"We didn't think of that, did we?" replied Yui looking at Natasha.

For the rest of the week, they amused people in their group by dressing in identical clothes and acting as twins. They even sang a duet of 'Sisters' in English at the farewell concert on the final night. It brought the house down.

Natasha applied for and received special permission to fly down to North Korea with her mother and the visitors and she too enjoyed the subterfuge, just as Yui had, which she had had no idea that her mother had been part of for the last few years.

As they hugged before Yui got onto the connecting coach back to the hotel, Natasha said, "That week went too quickly, Yui. You've got my address now, haven't you? You will write? We can be pen-pals! We just have to keep in touch, now that we have found each other. I couldn't bear to not see or speak to you again. I feel like I've found a long-lost sister. Good luck at uni".

Natasha was far more emotional than Yui's culture allowed her to be or to show anyway, but she did want to remain in contact with her new friend as well. "Our holiday has passed too quickly... and I know what you mean about sisters. It's funny, neither of us has any brothers or sisters... It is nice to have found one now... I'll write as soon as I get back to Tokyo!" she promised.

And she did too, and Natasha wrote straight back. Throughout the years, there was rarely a twenty-four hour period when there wasn't a letter heading towards one of them from the other one, unless they were already in one another's company.

In those days in the Soviet Union, wages were fairly similar whatever jobs workers did. What distinguished people was the amount of privilege they enjoyed, and Marina had a lot. When she announced her next 'cultural mission' to Japan, Natasha begged to be able to go with her. Marina didn't have the money to pay for her daughter's flight, but she managed to persuade the Party to pay for it eventually by convincing her superiors to endorse her request on the grounds that it would be useful training for Natasha in how to deal with the CPJ. She pointed out that if Natasha proved successful at negotiations with people in Japan, she could be used as a delegate to Communist Parties in those other countries, whose languages she spoke.

Permission finally came down and mother and daughter set off on an all-expenses-paid jolly to Tokyo. It was to become an annual event for Natasha, as it already was a bi-annual trip for her mother.

When Natasha officially joined the university of Alma Ata full-time in October 1967, she took Japanese Language, History and Culture as her main subject, but with English, French and German, and in September of the same year, Yui took Russian, English and Chinese. This meant that the Soviet state paid for Natasha to study in Japan for three months from January to April in her second and third years and the Japanese government paid for Yui to study in Russia in the summers of her second and third years as well.

They became as close as twins and even adopted identical mannerisms and ways of speech. Natasha had no problem imitating Yui's Japanese accent and neither did Yui copying Natasha's Russian, but they both spoke English differently – one English and the other American English. Natasha really didn't like the American accent and refused to use it, although she could do it if she wanted to, but Yui, like nearly all those who learn an American accent first, found a true English accent next to impossible to acquire.

When they were together, and after that initial meeting that meant between two weeks and five months a year, they were inseparable behaving more like close twins than friends. In fact, they were so natural together that few people they met socially ever found out that they were not twins and they certainly never denied it, because, as they described their relationship to each other and their parents, they were soul-twins to their way of thinking.

5 YURI VLADIMIROVITCH ANDROPOV

Both girls passed their finals with the highest distinctions possible, what in the West might be described as 'maxima cum laude', and after a couple of weeks of celebration with their families, friends and fellow students, during which they could not be together, they were turned out into the real world to earn a living.

However, again Fate acted upon them in a similar manner. Yui was granted the post in the Ministry of Finance that her father's bribe had bought for her subject to her results, and Natasha was allocated a teaching job at her old High School by the Department of Employment, until they could figure out how best to use her remarkable linguistic talents. Two months into her new job, Yui put in for two week's holiday to go on the 'August Kazakh Trip'. She would not have been granted it, but for the intervention of her parents, who could show that they 'always went away in August'. Hiroto had also risen to a position of some considerable influence within his department.

"Oh, Tash, it's so lovely to see you again! How are you keeping, darling?" she asked hugging her on the tarmac in the North Korean military airport. Hugging and kissing and calling her girlfriends 'darling' were affectations that she had learned at university.

"I'm fine, sister, and better still for seeing you, but you look sad, what is the matter?"

"I can't tell you now, let's just try to be happy. Have you got something to drink on that plane? I could murder a cold beer or glass of wine!" Natasha had also learned to drink beer at university, so they sat together on the plane, drank beer and caught up on one another's lives until they touched down in Alma Ata.

That evening they spoke again. "You're still sad, sister, why won't you tell me about your problem? We never used to keep anything from each other".

"It's nothing, really… I'm just being stupid… and ungrateful and I hate myself for it… It's my job, darling, that's all. There's nothing wrong as such.

I've been doing the job for two months, as you know, but it already feels like two years without a break. Just imagine, my parents have been doing it for…" she was counting on her fingers, "I'm twenty-two, and my Dad was doing it before the War, so that's… that's at least thirty-two years and my Mum a little bit less. It is mind-numbingly boring, Tash! All we do all day is add figures, subtract figures, divide figures, multiply figures and then check figures. All bloody day!

"Can you imagine that? It's driving me potty!"

"No, sister, I can't, but then I have chosen languages, as did you, so why are you doing it?"

"It's difficult to get a good job in Japan unless you know someone and my parents are in finance".

"Yes, I see… can't you transfer to a different department?"

"Yes, possibly, that is part of the plan, but first, I have to work in the Ministry of Finance for a year, I think Dad said. Then I can apply to the Foreign Office and eventually the Diplomatic Corps".

"Well, that's not so terrible, is it? You've already done two months, so you've only got ten months to go. Take courage, sister".

"I suppose so, but after another ten months, I may not have enough of a brain left to impress the Foreign Office recruitment board with".

Natasha laughed. "Your parents aren't stupid and neither are you. You'll make it, I know you will… Just keep your eyes on your goal and take one day at a time. This time next year it will all seem to have passed so quickly that you'll wonder why you allowed it to upset you so much".

"Yes, but that's part of the problem… You see, it's not only that, sis," she said automatically picking up on Natasha's term and dropping 'darling', "I don't want to be in Japan. What we have now is all I've ever known, but it doesn't feel like my country… I don't know how to describe it, but there is too much 'West' in Japan. The 'mix' doesn't feel right yet… I don't have anything against the West, in fact I wouldn't mind living there – the UK, Canada or the United States – but our hybrid is just a, a, a nothing! It's not Asian and it's not American, it's OK, I suppose, but it's false… and I hate it.

"You've been there often enough, what do you think of it?"

They had known each other well for four years since their first meeting, and could be honest with each other.

"I wouldn't want to live there either, sister. If I am to speak honestly, I think that the Americans have raped your culture as well as your women. They have acted like the cuckoo and are trying to replace your culture with their own. The resulting hybrid is not a happy one, as you suggest. They openly exploit the workers of your country or they do it covertly using the greedy co-operation of your corrupt ancient ruling class of wealthy, old-guard, imperialist families.

"All in all, yours is a sad, corrupt facsimile of America, except that the citizens don't receive the benefits that Americans get from their economy. The way I see it, your country is nothing but an aircraft carrier for them to defend their stolen interests in Asia, a land where they do not belong".

"Yes, well, that's roughly what I think too, but I am not under the illusion that I'll be able to change it, so I'd just rather get out and live in a rich country, make a lot of money and live my life as I want to".

"The temptation is great, sister, I know that, but it is greater for you than for me. I believe in the class struggle, and that the workers will eventually win, because we are in the majority and rich people cannot be rich without us. If we do not produce, they cannot sell, and we gain the upper hand".

"Yes, Tash, I agree, but I can't wait that long, I just want to enjoy a good life now. If it wasn't for my parents, I'd have buggered off already! I really would, but I know how much it would hurt them… and I would miss them as well".

"I would hate to see you disappear into the West too, sister, because I cannot follow you there at the moment. However, never say never, Comrade Brezhnev is opening new doors with the West all the time, so who knows what will happen in the future".

"If I had a good job in the West, Tash, I'd pay for your flights and everything. You'd never have to worry about anything like that".

"Thank you, I know you would", she replied covering her hand from across the table. "I just wish there was something I could do to help you, sister".

"There is, you could take my place at work! You could live with me and we could do a month on and a month off, the job pays well enough, and if not, well, the other one could work as a translator", she replied joking.

The following morning, Natasha told her mother about what had happened in her life the day before as she had done every day since she was a child.

"You have been to the den of American capitalist thuggery, where she lives, Natasha, but you have been shielded from it. Unfortunately, Yui is not. She is like a French goose being force-fed American propaganda in the form of nonsensical daytime television soap operas and relentless advertising, which is intended to turn the brains of working-class citizens into useless, non-thinking mush.

"This strategy usually works very well. The capitalist pigs have perfected their art to a high degree, but Yui has intelligent parents who have given her the ability to see through the smokescreen of International Capital. You have only encountered it in passing, so to speak, but Yui has to live in it like a fish in polluted water. Did you like what you saw when you were in Japan?"

"I will admit that I did like the wider choice of goods and services… and the cinema over there… I prefer it to ours".

"Perhaps, but we have been the subject of organised International embargoes! It is a capitalist ploy to sow unrest among the Soviet people. They have been trying it in various ways for fifty years, but our resolve to succeed is too strong for them. Anyway, the choice, as you call it, is only an illusion. You go into a Western supermarket to buy shampoo and you are confronted with a hundred different brands and types, but most of it is made in the same factories for different clients who stick their own labels on the containers and try to persuade you it is better than the others with advertising.

"In reality, it is not better, it is the same. Sometimes, the advertising and the packaging cost more than what's in the bottle and the consumer is made to pay for that without knowing it. They should be forced to say where it was made on the label.

"Anyway, the choice in Soviet outlets is improving, but ours is real choice. Soap made in the Urals, Uzbekistan, the Ukraine or here is manufactured to radically different formulas, not just one or two as in the West. Comrade Brezhnev, who has righted many of the excesses of Stalin and Khrushchev, is making remarkable progress in improving our standard of living, is he not?"

"Yes, mother, he is. It is better than even only a few years ago".

"There you are then, that is proof that we, the people of the glorious Soviet Union, even as we stand alone in the world, can succeed against the hundreds of other countries that have yet to shake off the yoke of capitalism".

"Yes, mother, I know, you are preaching to the converted".

"I am not preaching, Natasha! That is what the clergy lackeys of capital do. Comrade Brezhnev has pointed out the error of Stalin in re-allowing the priests to infect our ideology".

"Yes, Mum, I know. May I go to my room now to study?"

"Yes, of course, I have to get ready to go out now anyway".

"Oh, one last thing, Mum. You'll never guess what Yui suggested… she said that I should take her place… you know, go into work for her! That would be a laugh, wouldn't it? She was only joking, of course, but imagine that, me working for the Japanese Ministry of Finance. She's so down, but she can still make jokes. See you later, Mum, have a lovely day!"

"You too, Natasha. I will see you for tea, won't I?"

"Yes, Mum, I'll have Yui with me".

A few hours later, when Marina was enjoying a cup of coffee and a cake alone between lectures at a local factory, Natasha's words came back to her and wheels started to move within her mind. At first, the possibility was too enormous to grasp, but the idea would not leave her alone. It distracted her all afternoon. She was glad when her last lecture was over and she could retire to her office at the AACPHQ. She left instructions with her secretary that she was not to be disturbed.

Such a move was bold, and not without risk, but the rewards would be tremendous. It would guarantee her leadership of the AACP and may even gain her a commendation from the Central Committee itself, which would ensure that the right people had at least heard of her name. She ran over the practicalities, but she had no doubt that her daughter could pull it off. However, first Natasha would have to agree to make the sacrifice for the love of the Motherland and, dare she admit it, for the love of her mother?

She was a good girl though, she reasoned, Natasha would see the sense of the proposition, but she would have to discuss it with the committee first and make certain that everyone in the top ranks of the AACP knew that it was her idea. She wrote her outline proposals on a sheet of paper, stamped the date on it and got her secretary to confirm the date with her signature, then sealed it in an envelope and put that in the safe. After a few deep breaths, she went down the corridor to the chairman's office, asked his secretary if he was free and knocked the door.

"It is an unbelievable opportunity, Comrade Marina. I will readily admit that I am completely flabbergasted. I have never dealt with a situation that has the potential to be so momentous. Are you completely sure of your facts?"

"Yes, comrade, absolutely positive. You have seen the two girls yourself many times, do you not think they could pull it off?"

"Their likeness is quite uncanny for two unrelated girls from different countries, I agree. They are like two peas in a pod, but under the pressure of Yui's peers at work? That is not the same. It is a tricky one… Do you have Yui's consent to do this?"

"No, comrade, at the moment this is just speculation from a chance comment made by the girl Yui to my daughter. I wanted to consult you before taking it any further, Comrade Chairman".

"Yes, I see, that was wise of you. This matter has such huge potential, we must proceed with caution. How long has the girl left here?"

"Six nights, comrade".

"All right, leave it with me. Well done, Comrade Marina, I'll be in touch with you as soon as I can".

Marina left the office knowing that she had done the right thing, but wishing that she could have taken it over her old leader's head, as he would now want a share of the glory, despite the fact that it was too big an issue for him to handle. Perhaps it was time for another good, old-fashioned purge, she thought, so long as it didn't affect people on her status level.

All her senses told her that this was the boost to her career that she needed and she was determined not to let it slip between her fingers, no matter what.

When authorisation to proceed with the initial enquiries came back a few days later, the CPJ visit was almost over, but Marina took her daughter aside.

"Do you remember what you told me about Yui being so bored with her job that she suggested a switch?"

"Yes", replied Natasha, "what of it? It was only a joke…"

"Well, perhaps we could build on that… what do you think?"

"Build on what? I have no idea what you're talking about, Mum".

"Really? That is disappointing, but you are still young. Your friend Yui has a good job in the Japanese government, but she hates it. She has suggested that you take her place, correct? Now what do you think?"

"Sorry, Mum, but have you gone mad? Swapping identities with Yui for a laugh on a Saturday afternoon is one thing, but this? Er, what is this by the way, I'm getting confused here. I have a sort of an idea, but I want to hear it from you. What are you suggesting exactly?"

"Mmm, well, first off, I want you to know that this idea is unprecedented in Soviet history, so it is a brand-new concept. However, if you took Yui's place, took over her whole life, in Japan, you could feed us with their secrets".

"Become a spy, you mean? A female James Bond?"

"Yes and no… a spy, yes, a James Bond, no. You would just become Yui and she would disappear".

"What do you mean by 'disappear', Mum?"

"Oh nothing nasty, I assure you, but I'm sure that the Soviet government could find her a comfortable new life".

"Mum, I know for certain that Yui would not want to live here, she has her heart set on living somewhere in the West".

"Oh, I didn't know that, but just leave that with me, I'm sure there are ways and means", she said making a mental note to discuss the possibilities with the chairman in the morning. "I'm sure we'll be able to sort something out for her. The next step is down to you now, you need to raise the subject with her again".

As she realised that her mother was serious, the proposition hit Natasha like a slate from a roof, but she promised to talk to her friend about it as soon as she could

"I'm sorry, Natasha, but you can't just walk up to her and offer to swap identities. There is a lot more to it than that… Perhaps, you could talk to her about it in a jocular fashion… just say something like, 'Remember what you said about me going into work for you? I've had such a laugh about that. The idea tickles me. Do you really think I could pull it off?"

Which is exactly what she did. She could justify it to herself because she knew that Yui wanted out and she wanted in, even if it was only for the sakes of her mother and the Motherland. Her main priority though was not to abuse her friendship with Yui.

However, it was difficult. Natasha tried talking about it with Yui several times, but Yui didn't seem to catch her drift, so she sought advice from her mother, who did her best, but eventually took her to the Party chairman. However, he didn't have any clear advice either. A couple of days later, the CPJ contingent returned home with no progress having been made. The following day, the chairman called Marina and Natasha into his office.

"Please take a seat, both. As you know, this business with Yui is most delicate and I have to admit that no-one here has the experience to be able to offer either of you any meaningful advice. I have been keeping certain people in the loop, so to speak, and this morning, I had a telephone call from the Kremlin, summoning you both to present yourselves to no less a personage than Comrade Andropov himself in three days' time".

He picked up a telegramme from his desk. "Yes, here it is. You fly out the day after tomorrow. Just present this telegramme at Alma Ata airport and you will be taken care of. There will also be rooms in your name at the Moskovskaya Hotel near the Red Square. I'm sure that I don't need to impress on you how important this meeting will be. Comrade Andropov's reputation is well known. I can't say that I wish I was going with you, but I do wish you both the very best of luck".

Marina and Natasha left his office shell-shocked.

"Don't worry, Mum, if it was bad news, they wouldn't bother summoning us to Moscow, they'd just have us dealt with here".

Marina was still clutching the telegramme, "What? Oh, yes, don't even talk like that, Natasha! Everything will be fine. I have a feeling in my bones that this is good news".

∞

Neither of them had ever been to Moscow before, and they were a little in awe. The day after they arrived they presented themselves to the guard at the main entrance to the Kremlin on the Red Square. To be on the Red Square near Lenin's Mausoleum was impressive enough, but to enter the actual Kremlin near St. Basil's Cathedral was withering. They walked into the impressive building with the demeanour of serfs encountering the lord of the manor and were glad that they had no friends there who could bear witness to their servitude.

After passing through security and a body search with the new large-loop metal detectors, such as they had recently introduced at airports, they were led into a large room and told to wait, which they did, for two hours, but there were so many fascinating pieces of artwork around about that the time passed quickly. Suddenly, a small man with the authoritative air of a giant instructed them to follow him. They stopped at a door with the letters 'KGB' on a gold plate, and 'Y. V. Andropov' on another beneath it. It rang fear and awe into Marina's heart, despite what she had said, if not into Natasha's.

When they were invited in, they were glad they were offered a seat before their legs gave way, such was the man's fearsome reputation.

"Good afternoon, Comrades", he said standing to lean over his desk and shake their hands. "May I get you a drink? I know how overwhelming the Kremlin can be. Perhaps next time we will meet in my office in the Lubyanka, I feel more at home there too.

"I have a friend who sends me Johnny Walker Black Label if you would like to try it, or perhaps something a little less strong. Red wine? Comrade Ivan Ivanovitch, a small Scotch for me and two glasses of red wine for our visitors, please, then you may leave us". As the door closed, Andropov said, "Cheers. Now, I am told that you have a proposition, which will further the development of International Socialism".

"Yes, Comrade, my daughter here, Natalya, has a friend who is a high-flier in the Japanese Ministry of Finance, but she hopes to move to the Foreign Office soon. They could be twins, look, I have photographs. My daughter, the one on the right, is willing to switch identities with the other girl. Yui is her name. Yui hates her job and would like to move to America".

Andropov looked at Natasha over the top of the photographs in his hands with his piercing eyes. "Is this true, young comrade?"

"Yes, Comrade Andropov", she replied with a slight quiver in her voice, "but nothing is certain yet".

"No", her mother jumped in, "we would need approval first, of course, Comrade Andropov. We wouldn't do anything like this without authorisation".

"Yes, I understand that… and how soon could the plan go ahead?"

"As soon as we are granted approval, we can approach the girl, comrade, but she will probably have requirements, which we are not yet aware of".

"Yes, I see. Well, leave it with me. Goodbye for now, please return in four hours. You may either wait here or go shopping in the GUM on the corner outside the main gate. It is the largest department store in the world, you know, and soon we will have a branch in every major city in the land. You may go shopping now, if you wish".

Andropov started writing and Ivan appeared behind them.

"This way, if you please, comrades", he said and they were back in the corridor. "Were you instructed to wait here or look around the GUM?" he asked without any personal interest.

"We were told we could go shopping for four hours".

"Oh, good. This way, please". He led them back down the corridor, told the guard to give them return passes and put their names in the visitors' book. "It is better to be early than late", he advised, and then showed them out onto the square.

Marina's sharp sense of self-preservation told her to go shopping in the GUM or to at least have a coffee there, since that was what the powerful head of the KGB had advised and she didn't know whether they were being followed or not. However, she didn't bother explaining this to Natasha.

"Come on, Natasha! While we're here, we may as well take a look around the biggest shop in the world. We can stop for a coffee and a cake halfway around, if you like".

"OK, Mum, I'm up for it".

They returned to the main gate thirty minutes early and were shown to a bench outside Andropov's office. They were admitted as the clock struck five.

Ah, good to see you again, comrades. Did you enjoy your visit to the GUM and your lunch? I have not been there for some time now, because, well, to put not too fine a point on it, people would not leave me alone if I did, but I am assured that the food is still some of the best in the country and that means in the world, doesn't it?

"Please, sit down. A glass of red wine?" He served them himself and poured a double Johnny Walker for himself.

"Thank you, Comrade Andropov, you are most kind", said Marina.

"Nonsense," he replied graciously and then, "bottoms up to Comrade Brezhnev!" rather less so, but raising his glass with a smile. "It is just my little joke. You won't tell him I say it, will you?"

"Oh, no, comrade, never". The two women looked at each other, but managed to refrain from raising their eyebrows as well.

"Anyway, down to business. I have put your proposal to our beloved Leader, and he and his advisors like it. We all do, in fact. Congratulations! The plan has been given the code name 'Operation Youriko' You are to proceed in your negotiations with the utmost caution and to keep me informed on a regular basis. This is the number of this phone here", he said touching one of the four telephones to his right. It can be patched through to me wherever I am – at home, in the Lubyanka, anywhere at any time of the day or night.

"If I cannot take the message someone will, take a note of the name they give you and state your message. I may need the person's name, so write that down, but I would prefer that you both commit the phone number to memory".

Both women initiated the mental processes necessary and remembered the number, then Marina placed the note back on the desk. Andropov acknowledged it's return with a nod and a slight smile.

"Now, the nature of covert operations such as this, is that they are all different, since people and circumstances are different. Therefore, they cannot be managed from this office. However, we have hundreds of comrades operating abroad under very difficult circumstances, so your chances of success are high, young woman, if you keep your nerve and remember that you are doing it for the love of Mother Russia… and the Soviet Republics, of course," he added quickly. "I understand, Comrade Marina Antonova, that you head a cultural delegation to Japan twice a year and that the girl's parents are personal friends.

"Did you know, by the way, that until four years ago, I was the head of the Department for Liaison with Communist and Workers' Parties in Socialist Countries? That didn't include Japan of course, but it's the same sort of thing".

"Yes, comrade, to both questions".

"Yes, comrade, your work with the CPJ went a long way to persuading us to accept your proposal. So, finish your wine and go now, but keep me informed. You will need to keep your superiors in the CPAA up-to-date as well, Comrade Marina Antonova, but it would be better if you phoned me first, so that we can check the validity of your information. After all, there is no point in bothering your already overworked comrades at the CPAA with details they don't need, is there? So, you tell me first, and we'll tell you what your colleagues need to know.

"Do you both understand me, comrades?"

"Yes, Comrade Andropov", they replied in unison at once in the office of the most feared man in the USSR, the head of the KGB and the dreaded Lubyanka prison. No-one could afford to get on the wrong side of Yuri Vladimirovich Andropov.

"Good, well let's leave it at that for now then. It was charming to have met you. Oh, one last thing, Comrade Marina If this is some elaborate ruse to get your daughter to the West, there will be consequences, and they will be dire. I can promise you that many people will attest that I am a man of my word".

He started writing again; the interview was over, and Ivan Ivanovitch was waiting for them.

"Are you all right, Natasha?" asked her mother when they were safely outside.

"Yes, Mum, but I don't like it here. I want to get as far away from that man as possible and our little flat in dear old Alma Ata fits the bill just nicely".

Without committing herself to agreeing, she replied, "We'll have to stay here tonight, but we'll get on the first flight tomorrow".

6 OPERATION YOURIKO

It was obvious that the negotiations could not be carried out over the telephone or by letter, and since Yui was working full-time, Natasha would have to go over to Tokyo. There was also the delicate problem that Yui didn't know anything about the Soviet plan yet. Therefore, the first thing that Marina and Natasha had to do was work out every angle of their proposal down to the finest detail they could, whilst only having their side of the story to work with. They went through the proposal over and over again, each playing first one rôle and then the other. They knew that they had to be able to provide answers or at least suggestions for every single doubt and anxiety that the Mizukis might raise.

Then they learned their gambit off pat so that they would both be singing from the same hymn sheet.

They decided not to tell Pyotr about Operation Youriko just yet, but they did have to phone Andropov and arrange probably nine months holiday in Tokyo for Natasha grantable in tranches of three months. Andropov agreed and had his department at the consulate open an account for Natasha at the HSBC bank in Hong Kong. It was funded with a thousand American dollars a week from a trading firm that was owned by a Soviet holding company.

It was a fortune, but Andropov had no idea what ordinary people earned or how much the cost of living was in Japan. A thousand a week seemed to him to be a small price to pay for what the girl was willing to do. He wouldn't have gotten out of bed for it, as the expression went.

It was thought best that Natasha went alone, while her mother did more work on the project in the background. When the big day came, Marina accompanied Natasha to the airport and wished her nervous daughter good luck. "You'll be fine, don't worry about a thing. If it blows up in your face, just say it was a joke".

"Yes, Mum, I'll remember…"

"You're not worried about flying on your own are you?"

"A little nervous, not worried, but I'll be all right… it's just it's my first time travelling alone".

"You've done the route before. You'll be fine, now, give your mother a kiss and be on your way".

Yui met Natasha off the plane at Tokyo airport. "I thought you were teaching… it's lovely to see you again, Tash".

"Yes, you as well, Yui. I was teaching, but there was a change of curriculum and one of the lecturers in Japanese is being promoted to Moscow, so they're grooming me to take her place. They've sent me here so I can learn more about Japan and its culture. Isn't it great?"

"Can't be bad, can it? And you've got three months?"

"At least, but perhaps longer, that part is out of my hands really. Let's get my things to the hotel, then we can talk".

"You're not going to be staying in my flat then? I thought you would".

"I can, but it's best if I keep the hotel room… you know, me being Soviet, you being in the Civil Service… we don't want to make waves for you, do we?"

"No, good idea. You're not paying for the hotel either, I suppose?"

"No, not me personally".

They went for a meal, but Natasha didn't bring up the real reason for her visit, since there were still nine months before Yui would apply to the Foreign Office. They spent weeks just having a good time, and every morning that Yui had to go to work with a hangover or without having had much sleep, Natasha commiserated with her. Sowing discontent was her best opening game plan, her mother had advised, and it seemed to be working.

"If it wasn't for the Foreign Office light at the end of the long nine month tunnel, I'd jack it all in tomorrow!" she often said. It was music to Natasha's ears, so after a month, Natasha tried to raise the heat.

"You know, Yui, it's funny", she said one night over a meal and a second bottle of wine in a fine restaurant, "but there you are not happy with your job, whereas I've always been happy to live in the USSR, but now, I'm getting used to this lifestyle of yours, and I wish I could stay here for as long as I wanted. The thing is, one day they will recall me and I'll have to go home at a moment's notice.

"I wish I could have your job, you've joked about it often enough… you don't want it, do you? You could have mine!"

"You haven't got a job… but you could have mine tomorrow, if we could work out a way of doing it". They both laughed, clinked glasses and drained them. Yui topped them back up. "If only", sighed Yui, "I'd jump at the chance, but I couldn't live in Alma Ata all my life… no offence. I want to go to the USA".

"Oh, you've made up your mind now, have you?"

"Yes, the UK's too old-fashioned and Canada's too cold, so it's California! Here I come!"

"What a pair we are, eh? I live in Alma Ata but don't want to, and would love to live here, and you live here, but would prefer California… Interesting, eh? We've always been alike, haven't we? Same birthday, same outward appearance, think similarly, single children, we're both linguists… we're similar in so many ways?"

"Yeah, a lot of the coincidences are interesting, but the work aspect is bloody frustrating, not interesting, unless you have any bright ideas".

"Let me see… Ah, now that you mention it, sister, I might just well do".

"Well, go on, I'm all ears, but shout up another bottle of wine first".

Natasha explained her plan, in as much detail as she deemed appropriate for that moment, in a jocular fashion, but then let the subject drop when she could see that her friend was too drunk to pay attention properly. Natasha was also pretty intoxicated, but she paid the bill and got the waiter to call them a taxi back to Yui's flat, where they both crashed out without showering. When Yui got up the following morning, a Saturday, it was ten o'clock and Natasha was already sitting at the breakfast bar in a dressing gown drinking coffee.

"Good morning! How's your head?"

Yui plonked herself down on a stool and laid her head on her hands on the counter. "Oh, I feel like death warmed up… I need a hair of the dog, darling sister. Be a love and pass me a beer out of the fridge will you? I don't need a glass, but will you open it for me… nice and quietly. I don't think I've got the strength".

Natasha passed the tin over and took one for herself as well.

"Yui, I couldn't get out of my head what we were talking about last night… It kept me awake, what about you?"

"Cheers, Tash! Er, what were we talking about? It hurts to think… Oh, yes, the switch. Are you being serious? I thought we were just having a laugh".

"Maybe we were just having a laugh last night, but I'm serious now. What do you think, seriously?"

"Seriously' with this hangover? Er, at the moment, I'd do it. Every weekend it's the same… I go out on Friday night and get drunk to celebrate that I've got two full days off before I have to go back into that shit-hole, then I wake up on Saturday and I'm miserable that I've got to go back in in less than two days… and it gets worse every hour. My weekend is ruined by thoughts like: 'Only forty hours and I'll be back at my desk… only thirty-nine hours…'. It drives me mad. This is not the life I envisaged I'd have once I left uni. I worked hard to get there, then I worked hard for four years to get my degree and I'm operating a bloody calculator all day. I tell you, this isn't what I signed up for!"

"My life is similar, as usual, sister. My job is not so boring, but at least you have the choice of foreign travel, I can only go where I'm sent. You are much freer than I am".

"Well, you're welcome to my freedom to be chained to my desk five days a week and chained to a bar trying to get over the effects of it all weekend. Like I said, this is no life for me. Cheers! If you want my life, you're welcome to it".

"Cheers! But what will you do, if I take your place?"

"You really are serious, aren't you, Natasha?" she said, putting her tin down and staring into her friend's eyes.

"Yes, I am, Yui, I really am. Never more so, I want to live here, but you can't just up-sticks and move to California… what would you need?"

"I've no idea, but a job, money and a visa spring to mind".

"What if my Mum could arrange all that? I mean, I don't know whether she could or not, but she loves me and wants me to be happy. She's pretty influential too".

"I've always known you're a deep one, Natasha, but I never saw this coming. Do you really think you could be me?"

"Only with your help and support, Yui, but then I know that I could pull it off, given time. I'd want to make sure you're all right too mind. This isn't just about me, but I'm sure Mum could sort something out for you. Will you give me permission to ask her?"

"Sure, why not? I've got nothing to lose by asking".

Natasha phoned her mother from the Post Office, which they assumed was bugged and told her that she was excited to have been offered a new job and might accept it. If the conditions were right. It was a predetermined code phrase, and Marina lost no time in transmitting its translation to Andropov.

The reply that came back from Andropov was to 'offer her a million Canadian dollars, a decent job in the administration of a Canadian firm in Canada, and a new Japanese passport in any name she chooses'. He further pointed out that after a year of bedding into Canadian society, she would be able to move freely to California or anywhere else she chose.

"Take these details to her yourself, Comrade Marina, do not trust the post office or the telephone companies".

Marina got on the first flight to Tokyo the following day. She felt herself rising another couple of rungs up the ladder and noticed that Andropov had stopped using her patronymic, a sign of increased trust and intimacy she hoped, although she did not dare reciprocate the informality.

"I am so grateful you can help our Natasha, Yui. She will have a better life here and be able to further the cause of International Socialism", said Marina when they were alone.

"I don't quite understand, Aunty Marina, what is it you are suggesting exactly?"

"Well, Yui, it's like this. We can raise a million dollars for you and get you a good job in Canada, and a brand-new identity through the International Socialist Community. So, Natasha would become you, and you would become whoever you liked…"

"Anyone I wanted to be with a million dollars in the bank…? Wow, that's an offer a girl doesn't get every day. What about my parents?"

"They don't know anything about it, but they will have to be in on it, naturally".

"A million dollars, eh, but why would I want to work if I had a million dollars?"

"Well, that's up to you, but you would integrate more easily into society, if you transferred from here into a new job in Canada, and then, after say a year, decided to accept another offer in California. It would look more natural".

"Yes, aunty, I see what you're saying… and you could do all this for me, if I give my life, er, I mean my identity to Tasha?"

"Yes, I can do that".

The penny dropped in Yui's head.

"Doesn't that mean that Tash will become a spy and I will be betraying my country?"

"That is one interpretation, but not the one I would choose. Is this your country any longer? Who would you be allowing Natasha to betray? Not the Japanese working class, but the American imperialists and their wealthy Japanese capitalist lackeys in the corrupt aristocracy. These are not your people! They don't give a damn about you. They are not your people at all".

She had to agree, in her head at least, that they were not, although she didn't want to give voice to her agreement. Instead, she said, "A new job and a new life, eh?"

"Exactly, without any risk to yourself and considerable benefits, not to mention that my daughter, your friend and soul-mate, would also be given a rare chance to excel and lead a better life".

Yui looked at Natasha, but Natasha tried not to influence her one way or the other. Persuasion and reasoning were her mother's specialities and she respected her friendship with Yui too much to pull cheap emotional stunts. She remained both expressionless and emotionless.

"I'll have to talk to Mum and Dad first".

"Of course you will, Yui," soothed Marina sensing victory, "that's only natural".

The following day at the ministry, Yui arranged to have dinner with her parents after work. "I have something very important I need to discuss with you," was all she would say, and they naturally assumed that she either had a boyfriend and wanted to get married or, at worst, that she was pregnant.

"Come in Yui and be seated. I'll call for dinner to be served. We are anxious to hear your news. Your father and I have been like cats on a hot tin roof all day in anticipation".

"All right, mother, but once Miko has served dinner, could you dismiss her for the rest of the evening? What I have to say is rather personal".

Her mother did as she was asked and Yui told her story.

"But this is unbelievable!" exclaimed her father in a state of shock. "We thought you had met a boy and wanted to get married... we never dreamt... who would?" he said looking around for help.

"It might be better if Aunty Marina and Natasha explained in more detail. Do you want to do that now or tomorrow? They are waiting in their hotel for my call, but they'll meet you tomorrow if you prefer".

"Suzume, what do you think?" asked Hiroto. She looked at the clock on the wall. It was seven thirty.

"It is not yet late, call them over, let's hear the full story, so we may discuss it as a family and sleep on it later in possession of all the facts, but I am compelled to say that this is a great shock to me. I feel as if a huge rotten rafter has fallen on my head. None of it makes any sense to me at the moment".

Yui made the call and the two Kazakh women arrived thirty minutes later. They were offered tea.

"I imagine that you have some questions", said Marina. Hiroto and Suzume looked at one another.

"I do not know whether to laugh or to cry at that, Marina. It is so natural that we would have questions that the statement seems fatuous. What we have heard from Yui tonight has all but rendered us brain-dead from shock. I suggest that we speak openly and freely tonight, because a subject of this magnitude cannot be dealt with diplomatically within the bounds of civilised convention by novices such as ourselves. Agreed?" They all did

"My first question", said Suzume, "is how did this bizarre proposal come about in the first place?" The Kazakhs looked at Yui, hoping that the answer would come from her lips.

"I guess I must have told Tash a hundred times how much I hate my job, and one day she said that she wished she could help, and I replied, 'Well you can, you could go in for me'. Something like that, wasn't it, Tasha?"

"Yes, exactly like that".

"It started as a joke and just snowballed, I guess".

"So, it wasn't your idea, Marina, or yours, Natasha?"

"No, not at all", replied Marina and Natasha agreed.

"If I thought that either of you had planted the seed of an idea in Yui's head that would rob us of our daughter's company, I would feel betrayed".

"It was nothing like that, I assure you, Hiroto".

"Thank you, and you will give our daughter a million dollars, a job in Canada and a new identity in exchange?" asked Suzume.

"Yes, it is enough for you all to move to Canada, if you should so wish". In a reflection of Suzume's parents' reaction to moving to Hiroshima almost thirty years before, Hiroto looked at his wife and she said, "Tokyo is our home and we are near retirement age, we cannot leave here at our time of life". Hiroto touched her hand and smiled at her to show his agreement.

"Perhaps, you could join me later. We could all start new lives in a new exciting country". Hiroto smiled at her, but his expression said: 'I don't think so'. "Well, with that sort of money, we could visit each other as often as we liked", but Hiroto knew that that wouldn't last long either.

"So, we are to have a daughter by name who is not a daughter by blood living in Tokyo. If the subterfuge is ever discovered, are we supposed to say that we hadn't noticed the swap?" asked Hiroto.

"We could find an excuse for a family rift – an unworthy boyfriend, perhaps", suggested Marina, but it shouldn't really be a problem since Yui was planning to enter the Diplomatic Corps, so she would have been living abroad most of the time anyway. You aren't really missing out on much more than you would have, and we hope that she will stay here until Natasha is well and truly settled in anyway.

"If we plan this properly, the switch will not deprive you of one minute extra of Yui's company".

"Yes, I see that, she was going anyway, yes, that is true. What if Natasha is discovered as a spy?"

"I have looked into that, Hiroto", replied Marina, "Japan does not employ capital punishment against foreign spies except in times of war. Our government would simply arrest some of your spies in Moscow and exchange them. It happens all the time".

"Yes, I have seen reports in the papers from time to time… and you, Natasha, you are willing to run the risk of imprisonment until a suitable exchange can be arranged?"

"Yes, Uncle Hiroto. I think that this is a worthwhile project to try. I do not see it as an attack on Japan, quite the opposite. Yui and I have talked many times about how the Americans have hijacked your culture, so, this is an assault on American imperialism, which may result in weakening their influence in Japan and even Asia as a whole".

He nodded sadly, considering his own minor attempts at weakening the American grip on Japan. "Yes, I understand where you are coming from. From that perspective, our Yui's decision to leave is quite fortuitous for Natasha and The Cause".

"Yes, that's how we see it too, Hiroto", answered Marina. "Yui will want for nothing for the rest of her life and we will have an ear on American political aspirations as they are played out by the corrupt Japanese government".

Neither Hiroto nor Suzume could argue that that was not a worthy cause, because it was one that they still supported.

"All right, thank you Marina and Natasha for taking the time to explain these things to us, but would you leave us now to discuss them as a family, please? We will meet again tomorrow".

They parted company amicably, if sadly, but it was agreed the following evening that the plan should go ahead. The day after that, Marina flew back to Alma Ata to tell Andropov the good news and set the wheels in motion.

Andropov's Cuckoo

7 THE PLAN IS AFOOT

For the remaining eight months after the switch had been agreed by the Mizukis, Yui taught her friend as much detail about her life and her work, such as the layout of the Ministry of Finance, as she could think of. She drew sketches of her office, where she sat, who else used the room and their names, where her parents' offices were in relation to hers. She showed Natasha photos of office parties and identified her colleagues and told her their personal details that she was aware of.

Natasha, for her part, took up Chinese privately, but it was not difficult for her because people of Chinese ethnicity made up a noticeable proportion of the population of Alma Ata and she had always had Chinese friends at school. She found the tones fascinating. Yui already spoke the language, so for months at home they only spoke to each other in Mandarin. Yui also had to prepare for the Foreign Office entry examination, but she had no fears about that.

They both worked hard and enjoyed it. They were natural academics who just loved to be learning. Natasha could soon speak English using Yui's American accent which she had picked up from her teachers and the television and so Natasha learned it from the television and their daily lives also.

When Yui passed the entrance exam, she resigned from the Ministry of Finance and Natasha took her place at the farewell party organised by Yui's parents at a posh local restaurant. The contingency plan for if anything went wrong was to pretend that she was drunk and overcome with emotion and had to go home early. Yui's parents would back her up, but all went well, there being only one tricky moment, when Natasha forgot a close colleague's son's name, but Suzume rescued her from that.

"You must be a little tipsy, my dear", she had helped, "he has the same name as our neighbour's son". Natasha had met him and learned his name as part of her re-education, so she had smoothed over her gaff.

There was to be a month's gap between finishing her old job and starting the new one, and during that period they dressed and behaved as differently as they could, or rather Natasha continued as their Yui-Natasha hybrid and Yui changed into someone else. Yui became Chou Toshimichi. One evening, as Yui was practising writing her new name and formulating a signature in Japanese and English, they realised that Natasha needed to learn Yui's signature and handwriting too

"That was a close one. Somebody might have spotted if your handwriting and signature had suddenly changed!" said Natasha.

"How do you feel about starting work as me next month, Tash? Or perhaps I should start calling you Yui?"

"We'll do that later. I feel all right about it, I guess… yes, pretty confident. I've worked hard at getting it right, we both have, haven't we? And nobody in the Foreign Office has ever met you before, or at least, only the selection board, and I doubt that they'll remember every detail, but we're practically identical anyway, though I'm glad you thought of the handwriting, that might have given me away one day. How about you and Canada?"

"It'll be weird having to pretend to be someone else, but then you know all about that already… I'm telling my granny how to suck eggs. At least I won't be doing anything really illegal. I mean, I'll be rich, I'll have a new job and my employers will vouch for me, so why would the authorities or anyone else want to dig any deeper?"

"They won't, Yui, you'll be fine and so will I, but watch it! Less of the 'granny', we're the same age".

"I wish it was tomorrow, Tash… I wish the switch was going to happen tomorrow".

"Don't wish your life away, Yui. I'm going to need another month of your coaching after I take up the job anyway, like we agreed, and Mum still has to get your paperwork and money together. I know that she's on the case, there is no problem, but she still needs to dot the 'I's' and cross the 'T's. It won't be long now, sister, spend your time thinking about what we could have overlooked, and enjoying each other's, and your parents', company".

"They've told me they're going to stop the August Alma Ata trips, they don't see the point any longer, they're going to go to Canada instead!" she screeched with a huge smile.

"That's great, Yui! I knew you'd all cope… and in your holidays, you can come back here. There's absolutely no reason why you shouldn't".

In the meantime, Marina was in contact with Andropov every day appraising him on the status quo, the girls' mental states and confirming that she had received this or that order or document. At one point, she was required to return to Moscow.

"Comrade Marina, it is good to see you again. I have asked you to come here so that you can give me your personal impressions of the state of Operation Youriko in person. We have done all that we can for now".

"Thank you, Comrade Andropov. I think that the mental state of the girls is excellent. We are all confident in the success of this venture and we have everything we need to take it through to the next stage".

"I do hope you're right because a great deal relies on the successful outcome of this mission. Here is the girl Yui's new passport and the bank account book with one million dollars credited. She should book her own flight to Toronto, where the company will have found her an apartment. This is a letter of invitation to Canada to take up a permanent position as a senior administrator with the company in the letterhead. It is a Canadian company that is controlled from here via a holding company in Hong Kong, so she will have no problems, I assure you. We are very professional at this kind of work.

"Is your daughter all set?"

"Yes, Comrade Andropov. They have two weeks more, until the first of next month, but they are still rehearsing as if for a theatre play".

"Very, good. If you will let me have those documents back, I will have them flown to Tokyo in a diplomatic bag. You will of course be there for the Big Day?"

"If you wish it, Comrade Andropov, I will be there".

"Yes, a bit of moral support always helps, I don't want anything to frighten my Little Cuckoo at the last moment, but stay well in the background".

A week later, Marina called into the Soviet Embassy in Tokyo to collect photocopies of the documents to show Yui.

"You will get the originals a few days before you leave next month. We can't afford for you to lose them or get them stolen, but I do have these for you. A Japanese ID card in the name of Chou Toshimichi and a bank book in the same name with the same balance as the account you gave to Natasha. Is that all right?"

Yui agreed and from that moment on, Yui became Chou, Natasha became Yui and Natasha disappeared, and they addressed each other as such. They made many mistakes in the first week, but in general, Natasha was better at it than Yui.

One of the tasks that they had left to do was get a new doctor and a new dentist. Chou cancelled her relationship with her old doctor and dentist taking her medical and dental records with her ostensibly to 'pass on to her new doctor and dentist'. She had been with them since infant school and they were sorry to see her leave, but she said that she had moved and needed practitioners closer to her new home. They understood and wished her well.

Yui then started on the books as a private patient with a new doctor and dental surgery near her apartment and had full check-ups to begin her new medical and dental records. The physical examination proved to have been shrewd as the Foreign Office later wanted copies of her medical records so they could put her on their group insurance scheme.

"A thought, Chou. What is your blood group?"

"Type O", she replied, "and yours?"

"The same. That's a bit of luck! I know it's the most common in the world, but it's still a bit of good luck".

"It means that we are confident, self-determined, optimistic, strong-willed and intuitive people, but also self-centred, cold, doubtful and unpredictable workaholics".

"Pardon? Where do you get all that from? Is it some sort of horoscope?"

"Haven't you heard of Masahito Nomi and his theories on human science and blood type affinity? Some people just call it 'Humanics'. Nomi says that our characteristics are determined by our blood types. Ours are the same, perhaps that's why we get on so well and you can impersonate me so easily".

Natasha wasn't so sure, but didn't want to say anything to upset her friend in case she wasn't joking. Instead, she said, "Do you think your Dad could make your medical records in the ministry disappear? That would solve any little problems we might not have thought of yet".

"I could ask him. He's pretty senior… I'm sure he could do it, if he wanted to… so long as he didn't have to sign for them. It's worth a try".

When the Big Day came, Natasha, as Yui checked the small pile of documentation on the table against the list that she was asked to take in with her: ID card, passport (if applicable), driving license (if applicable), school and university graduation certificates, address of GP, list of past and current medical conditions (measles as a child), proof of address, address of next of kin (none). She pushed everything into a folder and put that in her large knitted shoulder bag.

"Well, sis, this is it… Time to go over the top, as they used to say. Wish me luck. I won't meet you for lunch, it might look a bit odd, but I'll see you in the Irish Bar as soon as I can after I finish… about five thirty, I reckon".

"OK, sister, you'll be fine, I know you will, but I'll be as nervous as a kitten until I see you walk into that pub. You had better go now, they don't like lateness". They kissed on the cheeks and hugged. "Oh, here's some small change for the coffee machines, nobody's ever got any". She shook a few coins from a pot on a shelf. "I collect them for work, or I used to".

With that, Yui went down to the street to catch the bus into work, like she had done on dozens of occasions on practice runs. She walked in through the main entrance and showed a security guard her identity card. He in turn handed her a pre-fabricated card with her details and a photo on a cord to hang around her neck, and asked her to sign in the visitors' book. A young woman then led her to a side room where about a dozen other intakes were sitting. She nodded to them politely and took a seat.

"We'll wait another fifteen minutes until two minutes past nine, then we'll go on up", said the woman in charge, "and don't look so nervous… this isn't the KGB or the Gestapo, we're the good guys". People smiled, giggled or chuckled at her little joke and she smiled back. Little did Yui realise that the head of the KGB was at that very moment reassuring the head of the entire Soviet Union, Leonid Brezhnev, that Operation Youriko had started successfully. The only person who knew her well who didn't know what was going on was her father, who assumed that she was 'doing something with the soviet Embassy and the CPJ'.

Eventually, there were twenty-one new employees. When they went upstairs they were shown two coffee machines and a room where they should wait. Minutes later, five people entered the room and took seats at five individual tables. They each called a candidate over for an interview. Yui was one of the first five called up, because she hadn't wanted a drink. She was nervous enough, and didn't want to have another excuse to have to go to the toilet. She allowed her nervousness to show because it seemed more natural. Luckily, no-one had a clue about the real reason for her state of mind.

"Ah, Miss Yui Mizuki, take a seat, please. We need to fill in a questionnaire for your files. Do you have the paperwork we asked you to bring?"

"Yes, Mrs. Masuzoe", she replied reading the name from her ID tag. They went through all the usual questions like name, address, national insurance number, et cetera and then Mrs. Masuzoe took Yui's documents away to have them photocopied. The whole interview took about twenty minutes.

"Thank you, Miss Mizuki, you're done here now, if you'll just go through that door behind me, a photographer will take some photos for your files. I'm not saying that you have to or need to, all right, but if you want to check your face and hair first, now's the time to do it. The male photographers in there don't give a woman any time to prepare… it's just snap, snap, snap to them, but those photos will be on your file forever".

"Thank you for your thoughtful advice, Mrs. Masuzoe".

"You are most welcome, Yui. Next, please!" Yui checked herself in the mirror in her bag then entered the door. Four photographs (left and right profiles, close up and full body) later, she was shown another door which led into a small lecture theatre. There were brochures on the desktop before each seat, so she started to read one while awaiting further instructions. The brochures contained information about the good deeds the Foreign Office was involved in abroad. The rest of the day, with the exception of an hour for lunch in the staff canteen, was spent in the lecture theatre learning about the rôle of the Foreign Office at home and abroad.

It was easier than she had dared hope. She wasn't even worried about them processing her particulars in some back room and discovering her true identity. She was confident that she was in, and that her files would soon be pushed into a slot in some obscure storage facility and forgotten about, and she wasn't far wrong.

When she arrived at the Irish Bar, she and Chou hugged like long-separated twins.

"Oh, I'm so glad you're safe, Yui, my stomach has been churning all day. I haven't been able to keep any food down. Are you hungry? Let's have a bottle of wine and you can tell me all about it". Yui opted for a cheese and ham toasted sandwich, but Chou had nothing but half the chilled bottle of Bordeaux Blanc. "Were you very scared, Yui?"

"No, I wasn't scared at all. Cheers! Apprehensive was more like it. A bit like when you start a new school, or any new job. The fact is, I was Yui Mizuki in there and no-one else. I found it a lot easier to pull off than I'd imagined. I think I know what an actor feels like now when she's in character".

"What did they have you doing?"

"Nothing really… fill in a few forms, have a few photos taken, and listen to a few lectures".

"Pretty much what they had me doing when I joined the Min of Eff. That lasted a week with us".

"Yes, they said something like that, then they'll assign us to our departments where we 'will learn the job from the ground up', so the man said".

"You know what that means, don't you? You'll be dog's body to all and sundry. I had that too. 'Yui, get me a coffee!' 'Yui, get me so-and-so's file!' 'Yui, shine my shoes!' 'Yui, kiss my behind!'"

"I can live with that for a while. You've got to start somewhere and there's less competition at the bottom, so bring it on! It won't last forever, it's just the way they do things, so I just have to accept it, haven't I? It was a good day, I enjoyed it, but I'm also glad it's over. I won't be so nervous tomorrow – that's a plus point".

The month's induction passed pretty much as Chou predicted, but that didn't bother Yui. It was exciting to her, not only because of the danger but also because the job itself was a challenge. She was learning so much that the time passed quickly for her, but not so for Chou, who couldn't wait to start her new life, even though it did mean seeing a lot less of her beloved parents. Marina spent two weeks in Japan in that final month: one at the beginning to see how things went with her daughter and one at the end so that she could conclude the Soviet Union's part of the deal with Chou.

The three women met in a private booth in an expensive restaurant one evening.

"So, it all seems to be going well, eh, Yui? Chou?"

"Yes, Aunty Marina," answered Chou and Yui nodded in agreement". No problems".

"Good, Chou. I have this envelope here for you. There is no need to talk about what you find in there, but I would like you to open it and check the contents, so that you can be assured that we have kept our side of the bargain, as have you".

"It's like my birthday", she said smiling broadly. She put a hand in as if it were a Lucky Dip at a fairground and withdrew a passport in the name of Chou Toshimichi with a twelve-month visa and work permit for Canada. She inserted her hand again and felt another book, but guessed what it was, so pulled out some papers: a letter from the head of personnel offering her the job, and a letter of introduction to the CEO of the company. Then there was a new motorcycle driver's licence, which she handed to Yui saying that she had forgotten she had that, and finally a bank book with the sum of one million dollars credited in it. She hugged it to her heart.

"Oh, my God! It's really happening! I can't believe it, I'm a millionaire! Yui, I'm a millionaire!"

"Please, keep your voice down. Yes, tomorrow, I will introduce you to the man who will take you to Canada. Tell him when you can leave and he will help you buy a ticket".

"Wait a moment! Aren't you coming with me, Aunty? I don't like the sound of going to a strange country with a man I don't know".

"We hadn't thought about that. Is it a problem?"

"I'm certainly not comfortable with it, put it that way. Can't you come with me, Aunty? I had sort of counted on you coming with me, I've never been anywhere on my own before, and having a strange man for a minder doesn't set my mind at rest at all… I mean, he could be anyone, couldn't he?"

"The problem is that it's not that straightforward for a Soviet citizen to travel to the West at the drop of a hat. I'm not blaming you, but I do wish we'd foreseen this hiccup earlier. I'd need a visa for a start. Look, I'll see what

I can do, but I can't promise anything. If the powers that be want it t happen, I'm sure they will find a way, but I'd better skip my meal and go to try to sort this out. So when do you want to leave?"

"I'll go whenever you can get away, if it means you will be able to come with me... If you say three or four days' time, then three or four days it is, or tomorrow, or next month. I'm easy, honest!"

"OK, don't worry about it. I'm sure we can sort something out. I'll see you both tomorrow. Enjoy your meal".

Marina took a taxi to the Soviet Embassy and explained her problem. The Ambassador spoke to Moscow and obtained permission to give her a Diplomatic Passport. They left on the Tuesday on the same flight, but not together. Chou sat with the Canadian man who had come to collect her, who turned out to be a very nice person, and Marina sat in first class on her own. They completely ignored one another until they arrived at their hotel, where they seemingly met for the first time in the bar after dropping their bags in their rooms.

To the casual observer, the looked like two Japanese women, probably mother and daughter on holiday. They were both in high spirits to be in Canada, both for the first time. Marina stayed a week to get Chou settled into her new job and nice, new apartment, which was near the city centre and all the amenities, then left for Moscow to give a full report on Operation Youriko to Yuri Andropov.

Andropov's Cuckoo

8 THE KGB

The first week of induction training was the most boring time she spent at the Foreign Office, but the new Yui even found that interesting, because she had not been taught much about what government actually did in the Soviet Union, so it was all completely new to her. It was followed by a month of file-keeping, which most people would consider extremely boring, as Chou had, but Natasha did not. She saw it as an essential part of her covert job to know exactly where every type of file was stored. It made her a joy to work with.

Most of the new recruits knew that they had been selected for the Foreign Office because they were exceptionally bright, so they found filing beneath them. After a week of it, many began to show signs of being disgruntled, but not Yui, as she should now be called. She revelled in filing, so she was well-liked by all the old hands.

After the month of filing, she was assigned to the department that concentrated on the Soviet Union, because that was what Chou had put as her main field of interest, however, Yui was already making plans to change her specialised subject to the USA. In the meantime, she used every opportunity to read what they had on herself, her parents and, out of pure interest because she had met him, Andropov. He held a strange fascination for her that was to last the rest of her life.

There was a file on Marina, but it only listed her as a frequent visitor to the CPJ, and as a possible agent provocateur. Pyotr and herself were referred to simply as 'husband' and 'daughter'.

There was a great deal on Andropov, so much so that she couldn't hope to read it all in a month at the rate of several paragraphs a day. She was interested to read in the quick summary at the front of the dossier that he was considered a likely successor to Brezhnev.

It put her in awe to think that she had met and shaken hands with the man who, the Japanese government thought, would probably be their next head of state – the most powerful person in the USSR.

Whenever she saw her mother, she gleefully passed on all the snippets of information she had uncovered. They were both aware that it was very low-grade information, but it was something, and she was still only a dog's body in the Foreign Office. She never knew or asked whether her mother told Andropov what the Japanese thought of him, but she figured that he probably knew he was one of those considered to be next in line anyway.

She worked six months in the Soviet office before an opening became vacant in the American department. The first thing she noticed was the atmosphere, because the USSR was considered the enemy, whereas the USA was the friend par excellence. She looked up the files of some famous names, but there was nothing in them that wasn't in the newspapers. Her problem was that she didn't know enough about foreign affairs to understand what was important. She needed more experience, which would come of its own accord, but for the time being, she had to have a project, so she asked her mother to find out which spheres of interest Andropov wanted to know about specifically.

Vietnam was the answer that came from Moscow via her chain of communication. So she remembered every word she heard spoken in the office on the subject and looked up every file she could find on it and made notes at home each evening. Her work was her life; she had no social life and no friends after Chou had left and didn't want any.

If her mother wasn't due over for a while, or she had something she thought was important, she mailed her information to a poste restante address, from where it was collected and delivered to the Soviet Embassy, but she preferred to give it to her mother in person if she could.

Natasha gradually got better at both her jobs, the overt and the covert ones, and after a year in the Foreign Office, she was selected to go to the Japanese Embassy in West Germany. She hadn't thought of that outcome in her plans, but she was sent there because she had worked in the Soviet department (and Russia supported East Germany), and the American department, (and America had arguably the most important sector in West

Berlin). She had been lucky, and her mother recommended that she take the job, which she did.

She was soon living in the first Western country she had ever been to and she liked it... even more than Japan. In the smaller confines of an embassy, every member of its reduced staff had to wear several hats. There was far more opportunity to read sensitive material and gossip was rife. The quality of the information she became privy too jumped exponentially, but it was more difficult, at least in her eyes, to get the information to where it had to go, not least because East and West Germany were home to more spies during the thirty years after the war than anywhere else in the world. Everyone was suspected of spying, especially foreigners and especially in Berlin and Bonn.

She no longer worried about being found to be Natalya Myrskii The Spy, she only worried about being caught as Yui The Spy. She had become Yui, Natasha no longer existed except in her mother's memory and the dark recesses of her own. After being in Bonn for a year, she had earned a month's holiday. She took a fortnight in Tokyo, where she met her parents, but didn't know what to do with the other two weeks, so she flew to London, for which it was not difficult to obtain a visa.

She loved London, especially Carnaby Street and she spent a lot of time on the phone to Chou, who was doing well and enjoying herself. She still had plans to emigrate to the USA, but Canada was not half as bad as she had expected, so she had delayed them 'sort of indefinitely for the time being', as she herself had put it. Chou hadn't asked where Yui was working and Yui didn't offer the information, it was better that she didn't know too much, although she did tell her that she was on holiday in London.

"Isn't it fabulous? I went there for my vacation last year. I'd go back again any time".

"Yes, I could live here, I love the fashion and the music", she replied, but when her holiday was over, she was glad to get back to work. It was hard trying to have a good time in a country or even a city where you knew no-one, it was also pretty boring as well.

Six months further into her career, Yui was being used as a special courier to take documents to the American consulate in Berlin, and smuggle sensitive material back to the Japanese Embassy, which would pass it on unopened to the Americans. It was a roundabout way of doing things, but it was the way things were done, sometimes, it seemed to Yui, just for the sake of it. Everything had to be done behind as dense a smokescreen as could be created. Transparency was most definitely not the word of the era or the Diplomatic Service.

Her job was nerve-wracking and dangerous, but exciting and rewarding. It was also intoxicating and addictive. She never looked forward to her holidays, but realised that she needed them when they arrived, because she would be mentally exhausted. She saw a lot of western Europe during her time off using Bonn as a base and once met her mother in Tito's Yugoslavia, where it was easy for her to get a visa as a Soviet citizen. Japan didn't object to Yui going there either.

One day, while visiting the American Consulate in Berlin, she overheard a conversation about an agent. The three men stopped speaking when they spotted Natasha in the doorway, but not before she had caught the agent's name. It was Andreas Schmidt and he was a double agent working in East Germany for the hated Secret Police or Stasi.

She passed the name back up her channels and a few weeks later she heard quite by accident that he had been found murdered in an alley.

"A warning to others", most of her colleagues had said sagely, since it was admitted in newspapers that he had spied for the Americans. It was the first time that she realised that the consequences of her actions could mean life or death for others whom she didn't even know. It frightened her to think that that man had only been doing what she was doing. She knew that neither Japan nor America would take her life for the activities she was carrying out, but she hadn't realised that her own people and their friends would.

The matter-of-factness with which her embassy colleagues expected something like that to happen to a Soviet double agent made it sound a common occurrence or at least the expected punishment for 'the crime'.

It was something that she would have to think about long and hard, because it shook her resolve and enthusiasm for her covert activities. It showed, and people noticed. She was a popular person, but did not hang around with anybody in particular, she didn't have a boyfriend either, but that didn't stop her colleagues asking whether she was sick or perhaps even pregnant.

She tried to put on a brave face, and filtered the information that she sent so that it didn't endanger anyone's life. Her Soviet controllers soon noticed that she was sending them drivel, and eventually asked why.

She was approached one afternoon on a day off in a German cake shop while she was enjoying coffee and a slice of creamy, cherry gateau.

"Do you mind if I sit here, Miss?" asked a stranger as he put his saucer and plate down without waiting for an answer.

Yui looked around, there were other tables vacant, but out of politeness she said "No, please do".

"Yui, isn't it?" he asked, "Miss Yui Mizuki?"

"Who are you?"

"You could say that I am a friend of your parents. I know Pyotr and Marina very well. In fact, it was your mother who suggested that I come to look for you here. She said that it was your favourite cake shop".

"How is my mother?" asked Yui catching on.

"Oh, she is well, very well, but she is concerned that you might have lost some of your former enthusiasm for your job. As you no doubt are aware, it took a lot of organising, a lot of work… not to mention a lot of money, a great deal of money to get you where you are today… enjoying coffee and cake in an expensive coffee shop in Bonn. It's a lifestyle beyond the wildest dreams of your former school friends, would you not agree, Yui? So, your mother is wondering whether you still want the job, or whether you want to go back home".

"Yes, I see, well, you can assure my mother that I appreciate all she has done for me and will never let her down. It is true that I have been off colour recently, but I have begun to feel better these last few days, so things will be back to normal very soon".

"I am so glad to hear that, Yui, and I know that your mother will be too. I do so prefer to be the bearer of good tidings rather than bad ones. Well, I will leave you to enjoy your lunch. It was nice to meet you, perhaps we'll meet again one day. Bye for now".

She sat there for two more coffees, but could not warm up again, he had chilled her to the marrow. She thought about the references to her mother and knew that she was meant to interpret it as her personal mother and her Mother Russia, which meant the Kremlin and the KGB in those days. She was glad to get back to work, where the man would not dare to bother her, but she dreaded going back to her flat at night, so she applied for one of the few apartments in the embassy on the grounds that a man had been stalking her. She was given priority, but the rooms were highly sought after, so she was told that it could take a long time.

She considered taking a lover just for the security, but didn't really like the idea Instead, she looked around for an apartment in a more secure block, although that would necessarily cost more. The head of personnel offered his assistance and she accepted it gratefully, but in the back of her mind she knew that she was only really safe from the KGB on the embassy grounds.

She kept a low profile though and sent all the information she could gather, it just didn't happen every day that she overheard a double agent's name. A week later, when she was starting to recover from her meeting with the man, she found a hand-written note in her mail box at her flat. It read: 'Your mother would like you to phone her here' and a number. She recognised the area code, it was Düsseldorf, but she didn't know whether the reference was to her own mother or the state, although she had to ring it anyway, she had no choice. She did so from a public phone box and was trembling waiting for it to be answered.

"Hallo", answered the voice, but it was female and did sound as if could be her mother, at least it wasn't 'him' - that was something to be thankful for.

"Hello, I was left this number", she said in Japanese, "and asked to ring it. I had hoped to speak to someone I used to know, a Natalya. Do you know a Natalya?"

"Yes, I do, but she's not here at the moment, perhaps you could come around tomorrow... she may be here then. Can you make that?"

"I will be there. Where?"

"Just go to the main train station in the city here, phone me when you arrive, and wait at the ice cream parlour near the clock. I will find you. Until tomorrow".

"Bye", she replied then hung up, but at least a minute after her mother. 'What on Earth was she doing in the West?' she wondered and went back to her apartment. She could get up at seven-ish, phone in sick, leave the flat at eight and catch one of the two or three trains an hour to be there by ten. It was only an hour away.

She phoned her mother, when she had found a good, highly-visible seat at the ice cream parlour from a phone which the staff placed on the counter for her. Her mother arrived twenty minutes later and Yui was pleased to see that she was alone. She sat down next to her daughter and asked about the quality of the ice cream. They hadn't had a hugging relationship since Yui was a seven-year-old Natasha, but she wished they did have at that moment. Yui was close to tears. They took their ice creams inside and sat at the back.

"How are you, mother?" she asked.

"I have seen better days, and you?" She looked tired, old and drawn.

"Me too", replied Yui, "I've been thinking of taking up smoking, or a lover, you know, for a bit of fun. I don't seem to get any these days... these years, I mean".

"Don't bother, I've tried both, they didn't help. They both cost too much in the long run. Cigarettes are a drain on your finances, men are a drain on your emotions, and both are a drain on your health".

Yui had never heard her mother speaking like that before, but then she would never have dreamed of talking to her about lovers before either, even in a joke. She didn't know whether it was a sign of her growing up or of despair.

"What brings you to West Germany, Mum?"

"Oh, a powerful man in the Kremlin and a young Japanese woman that used to be my Russian daughter".

"Yes, tricky".

"What's going on, dear?"

"Nothing... something just snapped when Schmidt was murdered and I was the one who'd fingered him".

"He was no good. He had lots of people arrested or killed, so don't waste any of your sympathy on him".

"OK, but next time I may make a mistake and an innocent person might die. I reported Schmidt, but on the flimsiest of evidence really, well, no evidence at all actually. I only heard his name in one sentence".

"However, you were right. They didn't just come over and assassinate him because of you. They checked him out first, and they had had their suspicions for a long time. You only confirmed them. They wouldn't go and murder someone just on your say-so. Think about it. If women could do that, half the men in the world would be dead". They both laughed. "That's better, you have a lovely smile, you should use it more often. You know, perhaps you're right about getting a lover. How long can you spare with me, Natasha?"

"As long as you have, that's not important. How about you?"

"I was only given a few hours to talk to you on my way back from a delegation. I fly back tonight". She was lying; she had been sent there via Yugoslavia to find out what the matter was with her daughter. She felt that she had sorted that problem out now though and didn't want to antagonise anyone in Russia by staying away too long.

At five o'clock, she saw Yui on the train back to Bonn, collected her things from the safe house and returned to the station to board a train to Belgrade, from where she could fly to Moscow without let nor hindrance. She was happy to have met her daughter even for so brief a while, but she was troubled by Natasha's apparent change of enthusiasm. She could see that something had indeed 'snapped' and she suspected that her daughter was not telling her everything, which would make writing a report for Andropov difficult. However, if he wanted to see her personally, she knew that she would not be able to keep her misgivings from him.

These worries not only ruined the flight back for her and she had always so enjoyed flying, but also kept her awake all night. She knew that if this change of attitude continued it would have serious consequences for Natasha, but it would also reflect badly on her. For the first time in twenty-odd years, she could feel herself about to slide down the greasy pole rather than being on the verge of another scramble upwards, and she didn't like it.

She didn't like it one little bit, so as she always had done in her life, she started to invent solutions to different scenarios. She preferred to be ready for the worst.

Marina was lying in her hotel bed in Moscow sweating, when she finally had to admit to herself what the final, worst case scenario could be, but it was to horrible to dwell upon, even for her.

9 THE DAILY GRIND

Yui's talk with her mother did her a lot of good, as short and as sad as it was. It made perfect sense to her that the massive Soviet machine was not going to swing into action to murder a man on foreign soil just on her suspicions alone. Her problem was she had no-one she could discuss these things with. It wasn't that type of job, but no-one had taught or told her that it would be like this and they certainly hadn't taught her how to cope with it. She had been thrown in at the deep end, the very deep end and told to get on with it.

It crossed her mind that none of the people she had met in the Soviet Union who had been involved with Operation Youriko had probably ever done anything like she was doing, so how would they know? She couldn't expect her mother or the chairman of the AACP to have anticipated it, as clever as her mother was, but she suspected that Andropov might have had an inkling, but hadn't said anything for fear of frightening his Little Cuckoo away.

It was an extremely lonely life. She thought again about the comfort of a lover, but she still wouldn't be able to discuss her real problems with him, and what if she talked in her sleep? That could be disastrous. It was too risky, she decided; she was doomed to a solitary life and an empty bed for the foreseeable future.

She was soon back to her old self, and wondered for the first time whether she had just been through a mental breakdown. A breakdown or fit of depression, she wasn't sure, but considered it likely. She concluded that she might be able to prevent another episode of whatever it had been by meeting her mother in person about twice a year just to have a little pep talk, so that she didn't have quite such a feeling of abandonment. Perhaps, she could send a card from East Berlin to Alma Ata direct, or from West Germany to the CPJ to forward, or maybe she would meet that man again. He had lost his terror for her now, because she realised that he was the only 'friend' she had in the West, who knew who she really was, what she was doing, and probably what she was going through. He had the potential of being her most fearsome enemy or her only ally.

She seemed quite far removed from Vietnam in the mid-Seventies and America had all but pulled their troops out of there anyway, so on her own initiative, she started to concentrate on NATO troop movements, because many countries had troops on the border between Eastern and Western Europe. Her decision was justified when Saigon eventually fell in April 1975.

She had had one man killed, she joked with herself, she just hoped she wouldn't start World War Three, then she was amazed that that had even occurred to her. It brought a smile to her face, and it felt as if her bout of depression had suddenly ended with her ability to think of and tell herself that joke without becoming upset. She was back, back to normal and focussed on the two jobs in hand.

Yui had a range of fairly menial tasks at the embassy as she was still considered to be in training, but she had moved on and up from 'just filing' to helping out at reception where people came to enquire about visas or trade delegations, or even more mundanely to ask about hotels and tours. She quite liked that aspect of the job though, because it was the only time she really had a chance to speak with strangers and just have a chat with normal everyday people.

She also helped out with the granting of visas to Japan. She was not involved in the decision-making process, but she checked that the application forms were in order and that all the relevant questions had been answered. If an application passed her inspection, it was passed up to the next officer who would grant the visa by stamping and signing the paperwork and stamping the passport. This was not usually done in the presence of the applicant, because the process took so long, so then it was often Yui's job to phone the applicant to say that the passport was ready for collection, or otherwise to post it on.

There were also a few rejections, but not many, and she wasn't high enough yet to deal with them. In short, her job was becoming more varied and so more interesting as time went on. However, the highlight of every month was the party or often parties. These were usually trade delegations, trade fairs or receptions held for visiting dignitaries from Japan and elsewhere. Once, there was a trade delegation from the Soviet Union and she had hoped that her mother would wangle an invitation, but she hadn't been there. Yui made a note to mention the opportunity next time she saw her.

She was usually invited in order to make the number of pretty women up. She knew that. Why else would she be asked to dress in traditional Japanese costume, when the men all wore western business suits? That didn't bother her though, it was all good fun and she enjoyed it. She met many famous people, while she was helping to hand out the sushi and canapés. It was the only social life she had.

Sometimes, the visitors were indiscreet or even downright rude, particularly if they got drunk and they were not accompanied by their wives. She had had her bottom pinched, slapped and fondled by senior politicians from most countries, but what they didn't realise was that Yui got her own secret revenge by passing the culprits' names on to the Kremlin as possible targets for honey-pot stings, where a beautiful girl would be used to obtain compromising photographs of important men for the purpose of blackmail.

She had no compunction about doing that, not in the slightest. She positively enjoyed the thought of these powerful men who thought they could get away with anything they liked, being humbled by a young woman with a pretty face. It became her most common useful information, as troop movements were difficult to disguise anyway and were routinely discussed in the newspapers.

However, the advances did not only come from visitors, most of the men working at the embassy had expressed an interest in her in one way or another. Some had given up a while ago, but others were more persistent. She played some of them along a little, she enjoyed the mild flirtation that often exists between the sexes in the workplace, but she wasn't interested though. It was just a way of getting along with everyone and amusing herself.

These names were also reported, she had no loyalty to them. Most of the men at the embassy were exceptionally polite and affable in public, but showed their true colours in private. They could be rude, machismo, and spiteful if they didn't get their own way, because they were spoiled, being used to getting what they wanted coming from the privileged backgrounds they did. Most of them were from wealthy, traditional families. They thought that Yui was similar to them and the real Yui was, or from the lower upper middle-class anyway.

She hated them, but could still behave properly and have some fun.

One day she heard some exciting news about a group calling themselves the Bader-Meinhoff Gang or Red Army Faction. She had heard of them before and read pieces in the newspapers about their activities, but the intelligence unit within the embassy started to take a much closer interest because they feared that the would link up with similar terrorist factions in Japan. Yui was able to tell Moscow exactly what the Japanese and therefore the Americans and the West Germans knew about the members of the Gang and their activities.

Her biggest triumph was being able to pass on transcripts from the Mahler and Stammheim trials, which were not made public because the court microphones were turned off and the defence lawyers were excluded from the court. The propaganda value of these documents was invaluable. She could easily justify her actions to herself, because she was defending the right of those men to a fair trial, condemning the fascist right-wing tactics taken by the authorities and promoting International Socialism.

She regained her zest for her work because she could actually see the help that her espionage was giving to the Red Army Faction and she was proud of it. She made the study of the RAF her own private hobby and she seriously swotted up on all its members and their activities both as reported in the press and as told in the dossiers in the embassy's files.

One Saturday morning, when she was not doing overtime, she finished her hamburger in a fast-food restaurant, checked the time, it was almost eleven, and phoned Chou from the phone booth at the back of the café.

"Hi, Chou, how are things?"

"I'm fine, thanks, Yui and you? It's so nice to hear your voice, when am I going to see you again?"

"I'm fine too, thanks, well, that's one of the reasons I'm phoning you actually. I think I could do with a holiday, and I can't think of anyone I'd rather spend it with than you. What do you reckon?"

"Great! Yeah, sure. When?"

"When do you suggest? I can put in my request for leave on Monday. I've got a month owing".

"OK, a month, eh? We could do a lot in that. Hire a car, drive about, fly down to California, Oh, Yui, you'd love it down there, I just know you would. Does that sound the sort of thing you'd like to do? We can do anything that pleases you, darling".

"Oh, yes! It sounds fabulous, when would be convenient?"

"Soon or not so soon?"

"As soon as you like, I could do with a complete break, I'm shattered".

"OK, for me to get a month off, and for you too, I imagine, we'll need to give a month's notice, so I can get away on the eleventh of June. How does that sound?"

"Perfect, I'm sure they'll let me go. It was only the other day that the head of personnel reminded me that I hadn't taken my holidays yet. The new rule is that if you don't take them you lose them, or get paid in lieu and taxed on it. Apparently my holidays expire in July, which is about right, that's when I was in London last year, remember?"

"Yes, that's right. Bastards, aren't they for threatening to take your holidays off you and tax you on them? It wouldn't happen to me, I love my vacations. OK, well, I know that this is costing you a fortune, darling, so I'll ring off now, but let me know what they say on Monday. Bye for now".

"Bye, Chou, and thank you".

As she was backing out of the phone booth, someone touched her shoulder. She started, let out a yelp involuntarily and spun around.

"Oh, I'm sorry, Yui. Did I startle you?"

"Er, yes, but it's not a problem, I was miles away… What can I do for you?"

"What could you do for me? Now that's a question and a half… I could dream about the answers to that for hours. Anyway, yes, I could see you were in a world of your own, I was watching you. Having a lovely, intimate chat with a close friend were you? You looked as if you were getting quite excited about something. What could that be, I wonder…?"

She studied the man's cold blue eyes and expressionless face with a false smile etched onto it. She didn't know what to say, and she knew that that was precisely why he had surprised her – in order to throw her off her guard.

"Why were you following me?" she asked instead.

"Oh, we can't hold a civilised conversation here outside the toilets in a cheap café, let's go to the bar next door where we won't be disturbed. Don't worry about your bill, your dear old Uncle Leonid paid it for you". He took her by the elbow in what appeared to be a friendly way and steered her outside and next door.

"What will you have, a cold beer? It's beginning to get so hot isn't it, and I hate to celebrate alone".

He sat down and placed the beers before them. "Cheers!" he said holding out his glass.

"Cheers", she replied touching her glass to his. "Why were you following me?"

"Who were you phoning? I asked first".

"A man I met at a party, if you must know".

"Oh! I was wondering when your hormones would convince you that you needed some male company". He leered at her. "We don't always follow you, just sometimes, at random. We like to have some sort of an idea where our most valuable citizens are. We would be stupid not to, you can see that, surely?"

She accepted at face value what he had told her and was grateful that he seemed to believe her as well, although she couldn't be a hundred percent sure of that. Her mind raced as to whether he could have the call traced, but she was certain that he could not. She began to relax a little.

"You said you were celebrating... celebrating what?"

"Your recent change of attitude and dedication to your work, my dear. What else?"

"Your sixtieth birthday?"

"Tsk, tsk, you offend me, or are you pulling my leg? Playing games with me, eh? That's nice, it means we're becoming friends.... I am forty-two, but I will admit to having led a hard life, perhaps it shows on my face more than I care to admit to myself", he said craning to frame his face in the mirror-advertisement on the wall opposite. "You, on the other hand, are as beautiful as the day you were born in your brand-new birthday suit, I'm sure. I can picture you now", he said staring at her chest.

"Thank you, I can't remember. You can ask my mother the next time you see her".

"Have I offended you in some way? If I have I assure you it wasn't my intention, but I do realise that when you get to meet so few genteel people such as yourself, you can become a little rough at the edges".

"In that case, you seriously need a six-month course in manners. I do not like being accosted; I do not like being followed and I do not like being dragged into bars by the elbow".

"Oh, that?"

"Yes, that!"

"I suppose I should practise being nicer when I am in such charming and beautiful company. I can't apologise for following you though, it's part of my job to follow your tight little bottom down the street. It is certainly one of the nicest parts… of my job, I mean, and if it wasn't mine, it would be someone else's turn. Better the Devil you know, eh, Yui?"

"You are trying to be offensive now, aren't you?"

"No, look at it from my point of view… Oh, that is very good! I don't mean your bottom of course, I mean my job. I am a red-blooded man and would rather watch your pretty little bottom in front of me than some fat man's arse. I'm trying to compliment you. You are a woman of the world, you know that men watch you".

"I know that dogs bite and bees sting too, but I don't need to be reminded of it by strangers. Thanks for the drink, but I have to be going now or am I supposed to wait for you to pay the bill, so you can follow me some more? I'll tell you what, I'm going down the road here to the outdoor vegetable market, you can pick up my trail there, OK?"

He smiled at her and touched his forelock as she scurried past him. Yui considered jumping in a taxi and going elsewhere, but there was no point. He could find her any time he wanted to, so she just did what she had told him she was going to do. Fifteen minutes later, she felt someone bump into her.

"Excuse me, Miss. My fault," said the man with a smile, then he turned and walked off ahead of her indicating that she wasn't being followed any longer that day… at least not by him.

She finished her shopping and then went home where she stayed all weekend, watching television and planning her forthcoming holiday. She was so looking forward to seeing Chou again and getting away from that odious man and his probably equally obnoxious colleagues.

On Monday morning, after collecting the post for her department, she went down the corridor to Personnel, knocked and walked in without waiting. It was very informal in the embassy out of the sight of the public.

"Good morning, Yui, a lovely day out there today, isn't it?"

"Yes, Michi. Could I see you about my holidays? Is it convenient now? Not to take them right now, just to talk about them and hopefully book them".

"Yes, of course, Yui. Please, take a seat. Wait one moment while I get your file. Would you like a coffee? I'm having one".

"No, thank you, I have to get back as soon as I can. Monday morning, eh? It's always busy, as you know".

"Yes, quite. Right, I have your file here. When would you like to go and for how long?"

"The tenth of June for a month, or is it four weeks?"

"Four weeks… the tenth of June, yes, that is possible, there are no important functions at which you will be required in the month thereafter… just a couple of parties, to which you would have been invited but not compelled to attend. Now, Oh! But there is a problem. A month from the tenth of June takes us to the eighth of July, and you have to take your holidays by July the first or lose them. That means you can have twenty-one days from this year, and seven days from next year's allocation. You will lose seven days for which you will receive seven days' salary.

"Is that acceptable?"

"It's not what I want, Michi, it's rather a disappointment. I don't want to lose seven days and pay tax on the salary in lieu".

"Yes, I can imagine, but that is one of the drawbacks of being a workaholic. Most people are planning their holiday for most of the year. This is not a common problem. Not a common problem at all. Rules are rules, they are there for a purpose and have to be obeyed".

"Yes, I understand, Michi. I'm not blaming you, really I'm not. It is entirely my own fault. In fact, you were good enough to remind me to take my holidays a while back. I should have reacted earlier".

He nodded his appreciation at the compliment.

"How about if I leave eight days earlier? I know that it's a lot less notice, but will that work, Michi, please?"

"Let me see, you are entitled, that is no problem and the diary says… er, no, there is nothing directly affecting you from the third, or the second or the first. In fact, you are clear of official functions in the whole of June, not that it is not always a pleasure to see you in attendance".

She raised a hand to her face to cover a blush that she thought probably wasn't there, caught his eye, smiled coyly and then looked away.

"So, does that mean I can leave earlier, Michi, and keep my full entitlement for next year?"

"Yes, it certainly does, if you are back from your holidays and in work by the first of July".

"May I see the calendar, please, Michi. Oh, this is fortuitous. Look at the weekends. I can finish work on Friday the thirtieth, leave on Saturday the thirty-first but start my holidays on June the second, and return on June the thirtieth. That is perfect. Thank you for your help, Michi".

"My pleasure, Yui. May I ask where you are going?"

"I think a fortnight on the Mediterranean, the South of France, perhaps and a fortnight in London, like I did last year".

"I hope you have a wonderful time. Might I suggest that you sort your visa for Britain out before you finish work. It will save you time".

"Good advice. Thanks again, I'd better go now".

That evening, she went to a coffee shop to phone Chou with the news.

"Did you get your holiday sorted out, Chou?"

"Yes, it starts on the eleventh, as we arranged. How about you?"

She didn't remember that an arrangement had been made, she thought they were feeling their employers out, but she didn't want to embarrass her friend so she said, "Yes, I'm set for the eleventh too, I'll see you then. I'm so looking forward to this. Start making plans, I'll go anywhere you want to take me, dear Chou. I haven't been looking forward to anything so much for ages and ages. Bye for now". She wanted to keep it short in case she was being watched.

Andropov's Cuckoo

10 THE HOLIDAY

Yui undertook certain arrangements before her holiday. She made a point of telling everyone who was interested that she was going to Les Calanques on the French Riviera for two weeks of her holidays and then she was going to London and she asked Michi to help her fool the concierge at her apartment block that she was not going away at all.

"I'm worried that he might go mooching around my flat if he knows I'm going to be away for so long, so would you help me?" she asked him.

"What do you have in mind?"

"Well, I could leave a suitcase with him and say that it's for the charity shop and that it will be collected. You come around when you have time between Thursday afternoon and Friday evening and pick it up. Then, if you would be so kind, you can either bring it to me in a coffee shop or perhaps give me a lift to the airport. That way he won't know I'm gone. I could be sick. There are three concierges anyway, so they might never know, but nobody will be able to say they saw me leave with a suitcase".

"Sure, I can do that for you, Yui. What time do you have to be at the airport?"

"Not until ten, the flight is at midnight".

"Yes, sure. I'll pick it up on Thursday in my lunch break, if you'll make sure it's there and I'll pick you up wherever you say on Friday and take you to the airport".

"Thanks, Michi", she had said kissing him on the cheek, "I knew I could rely on you".

It had all gone smoothly and she had taken many precautions to ensure that she was not followed to the bar she eventually chose to meet Michi in.

On arrival at the airport, she had put her carry-on case into a locker and ordered a business class return to Canada.

"It's a mighty big place, Miss, where do you want to go to exactly?"

"I don't mind, I'm just going for a look around, it's a spur-of-the-moment thing. I just don't want to have to wait. Which is the next flight you can get me on?"

"Er, let me see... two fourteen am to Ottawa".

"That'll do, but can you put me on standby for anything sooner?"

"Sure".

"Good, any class but first will do. I'll ride with the dogs in the kennels if it'll get me out there sooner".

"Certainly, Miss, keep your eye on the Air Canada notice board".

She had arrived in Ottawa at six pm after an eighteen hour flight and was certain that no-one but the receptionist and the bellhop knew where she was.

She spent the next nine days looking around Ottawa, but she was not really interested – she had far too much on her mind to play the tourist, when she was sure that no-one was watching. Some days she just stayed in the hotel, swam in the pool and watched television. She was only killing time and hoping that she wouldn't feel that cold hand on her shoulder from 'the man' or any of his friends.

If people like him ever had any friends.

On the ninth, she flew to Toronto, but she did feel a lot more vulnerable there, because too many people knew it was where her best friend lived. It was something that had only occurred to her on the plane, although she wasn't doing anything wrong. She wondered if she were becoming paranoid. Still, if they were going to catch up with her it would be there. She phoned Chou as soon as she could after landing.

"Hi Chou, I'm here. What's the plan, are you going to pick me up or where shall I get a taxi to? I don't like it here, I feel too exposed".

"You're paranoid, Yui, this is Canada, you're safe here. Not done anything wrong already have you?"

"No, but old habits die hard..."

"All right, I can pick you up, but it'll be forty-five minutes, if you really want to get away quickly, you're better off taking a taxi".

"OK, taxi it is. Where am I going?"

Just under an hour later they were hugging in Chou's apartment.

"It's gorgeous, Chou, the most beautiful apartment I've ever been in by far.

They stayed in that evening and caught up, discussing their jobs, their families and their love lives. Chou's appeared to be the exact opposite of Yui's.

"Why do you seem to be so nervous, Yui? I can't understand it".

"It's the life I lead, it's driving me crackers. I've got the bloody KGB paying for my hamburgers and buying me drinks, following me about, trying to put the frighteners on me".

"Sorry, sister, but it looks like they're succeeding. Why do they want to do that?"

"It's just their way of reminding me who's in charge. It wouldn't matter what I did for them, they'd still pull these silly stunts, but you're right, they wear you down, they do get to you, or they do to me. It's not like a normal job, you know, there's no-one I can call, no-one I can complain to. There is no International Union of Spies". They both laughed at her suggestion. You can't share anything, that's the worst part – the sheer loneliness".

'So, why are you frightened that they will follow you here?

"Paranoia, like you say. I didn't clear this holiday with them and told everyone I was going to the South of France".

"So you changed your mind, that's not a sin, is it? You're not actually doing anything wrong, are you?"

"Who knows what they think? I should imagine that I've broken some rule or other, not that they give you a rule book. The thing is, if they start looking for me, this is an obvious place to come to, isn't it?"

"Yes, I see your predicament. Well, no problem, we can fly down to California tomorrow. How does that sound".

"Brilliant".

They weren't sure about the validity of Yui's visa for the United States, so they hired a car, took a leisurely six hour drive around the western shoreline of Lake Ottawa and then crossed the US border into Buffalo, from where they took a flight to Los Angeles. They spent three weeks having the time of their lives as twin sisters. Chou spent money like water, paying for everything that the hopeful men around them didn't pick up the tabs for.

One evening, sitting on the veranda of their hotel suite overlooking San Francisco Bay, Chou sighed, "This is all going to come to an end soon, Yui, I'm afraid. Our holiday's just about up. We can fly back to Canada – you've got a visa for there - and if the American customs start moaning, just plead ignorance. We drove down, didn't think there'd be a problem and now we're going home. They won't make waves. Don't worry. If they say anything at all, they'll tell you you've been a naughty girl and send you on your way".

"I'm not going back, Chou".

"Really, there won't be a problem, trust me..."

"I'm not going back, it's not that I don't trust you, I'm just not going back to my old life. I've had enough. I can't do it any longer".

"But... er, how are you going to manage... I mean, I'll help in any way I can, but, what will you do?"

"I came here on a false passport. Look..." she rummaged in her handbag. "See? I made it myself, it's virtually undetectable since I made it in the embassy from genuine, original materials. They would only know it's false if they do a really thorough search. I even entered the number and my false name in the 'Passports Issued Log'. I'll find work, I'm not worried about that..."

"Aki Yamamoto?"

"Yes, catchy, isn't it?"

"Er, yes, lovely, but I wasn't talking about work, I've got heaps of money... I just mean, what will you do?"

"About what?"

"I don't know, will they let you just walk away or will they come after you?"

"I don't know, no idea... probably, but they might not. I've seen that they like to teach people lessons as warnings to others. I could defect in Canada and do something. They won't offer me a job in your place though, that much is for certain. There's something else I haven't told you, but only because I didn't want to spoil your holiday. I actually left Bonn on the thirtieth of May, and started my twenty-eight days holiday on June the second. I should have started work again on the first of July, so I am now absent without leave..."

"AWOL for three days, but where were you?"

"I was only in Ottawa, I stayed there just over a week. It was very relaxing actually".

"You're full of surprises, Yui, there's never a dull moment with you around. If you're going to defect, I think you ought to do it as soon as possible, don't you? At the moment, you are completely defenceless without police protection or whoever it is who protects defected ex-spies. Let's get out of here tomorrow morning, yeah?"

"I think that's a good idea".

∞

When Yui didn't report for work on July 1st, Michi was worried because it was so unlike her, but there was nothing he could do. She had to be missing for ten days before the police would react officially. However, he did know people with some influence and they checked the hospitals, police stations and morgues around Marseilles and London with no results.

However, the man, Colonel Vasily Dmitrievich Temko of the Komitet Gosudarstvennoy Bezopasnosti, the KGB, had more direct methods. Yui was to be followed every other Saturday from her flat, and from the embassy at least once a week. Four operatives took part in the routine surveillance of her and several dozen others. When nobody had seen her for two weeks, a report went back to Moscow and KGB officers were alerted in Toronto, Alma Ata and Tokyo.

Marina was interviewed, and surveillance was posted at Yui's flat, Chou's apartment and the Mizukis' house in Tokyo. When this revealed nothing, Marina was sent to Japan to talk to the Mizukis.

"Suzume", asked Marina sipping tea in her house, "I need to find my daughter. Something has happened, is she with Chou?"

"Yes, I think so. They went to California together a few weeks ago. I hope nothing serious has happened".

"No, well, we don't know, it's just that there is a suspected water leak in her flat and they need a key. Do you have a phone number for them?"

Suzume gave her the number and Marina left. She passed it to the embassy who sent it to Moscow, where it was cross checked and the name of the hotel discovered. A local team of KGB operatives was dispatched immediately, but as they arrived, Chou and Yui were boarding a taxi for the airport, although neither party noticed the other.

The surveillance team posted outside Chou's apartment noted their arrival at eight twenty-three am on Saturday the fifth of July, 1975. They sought permission to enter the building and apprehend Yui, but they were told to just sit and wait until she came out of her own accord, which they did at ten thirty on their way to the central police station, so that Yui could hand herself in.

Chou was knocked to the ground unconscious and Yui was bundled into a van and driven off. They later transferred to a Mercedes, which took her to a private airport and a private jet, which flew her to Leningrad, from where she was flown to Moscow after refuelling.

She was first taken to a police holding cell, where she was allowed to tidy herself up as best she could. The police officers at the station were used to dealing with scum, as they called them, but this young woman, who appeared to be of Japanese decent was well-spoken and didn't seem to fit the category, although it was clear that she had to have been detained for some reason. They treated her as nicely as they felt they could without risking upsetting anyone superior, because she was young and pretty.

Yui accepted a shower and her comb. She did what she could and took her make-up off. She felt a little better, but no amount of washing could remove the memory of what they had done to her in the aircraft. She had been stripped naked and every man on board except the pilot had inspected her for hidden weapons and contraband. Every orifice hurt, but not as much as her pride.

Those men had been worse than animals, at least these officers were trying to treat her like a human being with some respect. They left her to her own devices in her cell overnight, but they did not attempt to abuse her.

The following morning, after what passed for breakfast, she was handcuffed and taken to a place she recognised well. It was the most feared institution in the whole of the USSR, and there were many places to be afraid of, the dreaded Lubyanka, the home of the KGB, with its own special little prison on the ground floor. This was Andropov's lair. Sure, he had an office in the Kremlin, but this was where he was Tsar, where he ruled supreme.

It was no less than she had expected, although she had hoped against hope none the less.

She was led in through the prison and up to Andropov's third-floor office, which she waited outside under armed guard until they summoned her. She was scared, but there was nothing she could do about the situation.

A small green light came on above the door and she was taken in. Andropov sat behind his highly polished, dark mahogany desk with a leather inset, writing and her mother sat to the right-hand side of it. She looked even more tired and drawn than the last time she had seen her. She didn't look up from studying her hands in her lap. She looked like an embarrassed schoolgirl who had been caught shoplifting waiting for her father to give her a piece of his mind.

A rough hand on her shoulder stopped her two metres before the desk – a cold-looking, hard-backed chair between her and it. A moment later the head of the KGB looked up and nodded. The guards departed, leaving the three of them alone as in the past, but with Oh-such a different atmosphere. If she had found it intimidating before, she found it menacing now. Andropov was obviously waiting for his men to leave and the tension to build.

"Why have you done this to me, Natalya?" She noticed immediately, as all Soviets would, that he was using neither the polite patronymic, nor the universal 'comrade'. He obviously no longer considered her one of his comrades, if he ever had. "Haven't I always treated you and your mother with the utmost kindness and respect? I even took you to my heart and thought of you as my Little Cuckoo… it was my private, pet name for you".

"I couldn't take it any longer… it was so terribly lonely. I had no-one I could…"

Stop whining! Do you think I can go home and chat to my wife about my day in the office? 'Hello, darling?' 'Hello, darling, had a good day at the office?' 'So, so, darling, one spy was shot in China, we might be going to war with the Afghans, if the Americans don't keep out of there, but at least Leonid was in a good mood all day'. Do you think that your mother can go to the pub after work and talk about her job? Of course it was a lonely job! All the most important jobs are lonely jobs! Couldn't you see that before you started it?

"So, I'll ask you again, why did you try to run away?"

"I was weak and foolish", she said quietly, avoiding his eyes although she could feel them glaring at her.

"So, you were 'weak and foolish' were you? Or were you enticed away? That is a very serious crime against the state. It is treasonous, and treason is punished most severely. Do you realise how you have made your mother and me look to our colleagues and superiors? Do you realise what an embarrassment you have been to all those of us who placed their trust in you?"

"It was a moment of madness, Comra... Sir. I don't know what came over me". Her head still hung low, but she dared a sideways glance at her mother, who was also looking at her with her head bowed. Natasha had hoped to see some warmth, but there was only resentment. It bordered on hatred in its intensity. Natasha looked away again.

"I don't like liars, Natalya, take a tip from me: you are not in a good position to be lying to a man like me. You planned your defection for weeks. You created a false Japanese passport for yourself, this one, in fact, in the name of one Aki Yamamoto. Then you applied for a visa to Canada in that name. Those are not the actions of temporary, sudden insanity. They are the actions of a devious, scheming, little traitor.

I cannot tell you what a disappointment you are to us, Natalya. I am a man of few words, but I brood. I brood on things that upset me and emotions build up in me like steam in a kettle and then BANG!

"I take action, one way or another. Sometimes, I surprise even myself with the intensity of emotion that builds up in me. It is frightening, what I can do, and no-one will ever tell me off, or criticise me or even care. This is my home, my fortress, and here I am Tsar.

The steam is building up for you, Natalya, I can feel it, but I don't yet know how it will express itself and who else it will scald. Perhaps your mother or even both your parents... Who knows? Why should they continue to prosper when their daughter has cost the state so much money?

You will be put on trial, of course, but I can guarantee that you will go to prison for a very long time, and while you are there we will make you work off some of the money we spent on your lavish education, expensive trips to Japan and all the other privileges you enjoyed because of your mother's position within the Party, which brings me to you, Marina Antonova??

"What are we going to do with you? You have shown remarkably bad judgement and we can't have Party leaders who display a tendency to bad judgement, can we? Perhaps you shouldn't even be in the Party at all What do you think, Marina Antonova, should we expel you from the Party and get you a job sweeping the streets?"

"I am in your hands, Comrade Andropov, but I did give you my best assistance at all times…"

He looked at the top of Marina's head for a long moment, then walked over to Natasha.

"Do you think that your mother gave us her 'best assistance at all times', Natalya?"

"Yes, Sir, I am sure that she did… she has always been devoted to the Party and the Motherland", she replied trying to compensate for some of the problems she had unwittingly brought down on her mother's head.

"Well, I'm not so sure, but perhaps you're right. After all, she was the one who told us where we could find you. Not many mothers would do that to their own daughters for their country, would they, Natalya? It must say something about the kind of woman she is… the kind of mother she is".

Andropov toed a button on the floor and the guards re-entered the room.

"Take them down, separate cells, solitary for the girl", but Natasha didn't feel them take her away, she didn't even feel her head hit the cold, damp, stone floor when they threw her into the dark cell. Her brain wasn't working any more.

Andropov's Cuckoo

11 LUBYANKA

It was a bitter thing to know that her own mother had sold her out in order to mitigate her own sentence, which she hadn't deserved anyway, because Marina had only ever tried to promote the interests of the Party and the Motherland, even if her motivation was ultimately her own self-promotion. However, that was the way the system worked. She had brought strife down on her family, because they would be used to teach others a lesson.

If Natasha had felt lonely before, she hadn't realised what true loneliness was, she had not had the faintest notion. At least when she had been lonely on the outside, she could see and talk to people, even watch television, but in solitary, she had absolutely no-one and nothing. Furthermore, the Lubyanka was a Victorian building that had been commandeered by the Party shortly after The October Revolution, since when it had always housed the Secret Service, better known by its initials, the KGB, and almost from the start they had converted the ground floor into a prison. That had been fifty years ago, and no money had been spent on improving conditions for the inmates ever since.

The prison and especially the solitary confinement cells were damp and cold. Natasha had only two reference points during the day, but she didn't know what time of day they signified, although they seemed to her to be regularly spaced. At one point, a ladle of stew and a lump of bread would be put into her plate, which had to be waiting by the shutter at the foot of the door. At the other there would be a knock on the door at head-height and someone would shout 'Are you alive?' to which she would reply, 'Yes'.

Sometimes, they would make a joke along the lines of 'Are you dead yet? Is that your rotting corpse I can smell or your shit bucket?' All attempts at conversation were rebuffed. She knew that all too well, because in the beginning of her imprisonment she had tried to strike up conversations with the guards, but they would either ignore her or laugh at her. If she persisted, she got a slap. She had received a few of those and then learned her lesson.

The highlight of the week was for the door to be opened so she could clean her cell and empty her bucket. Then she was back to complete and utter darkness. To give herself a sense of time, she counted the visits. At one point she was worried that she couldn't remember whether she had been there for two bucket changes, two meals and one body count or two bucket changes, one meal and two body counts. It upset her so much that she spent hours calculating and recalculating. She eventually settled for remembering the divisions of her timepiece as two words, two words, one word: bucket changes, body counts, meals, which translated into weeks, mornings and afternoons or at least she thought they did, but it didn't really matter. At least it gave her something to do, a sense of time, no matter how wrong she was.

In the early days, sitting on the stone floor, she had blamed her mother for her predicament, although she had never cursed her or wished her any harm, but as time wore on, she was able to see that she had brought all her misfortune upon herself and she had upset the lives of her mother and her completely innocent father too. The most useful way she had found of keeping her mind busy though was to start with the first word in the dictionary she could think of and try to translate it into all the languages she had learned and more by guessing what it would be in Italian and Croatian.

At other times, she would sing songs from her childhood quietly or listen to other prisoners talking to one another or just screaming loudly to their Maker. There was a lot more screaming than talking, so she didn't dare try make herself known to the other inmates, but she would lie on the stone floor with her ear to the crack under the door and listen. Sometimes she heard no voices for a long time, and sometimes it was a long, long time, but there was always some sound, boots on stone, simpering, sobbing, screaming, shouting or whispering.

It made her fearful that it had to be her turn soon, but they never came for her. It was like being on a narrow ledge of rock at great altitude, she was constantly in fear of falling off.

At the time of five bucket changes, four body counts and three meals, Natasha's door was flung open.

"Right, Natalya Petrovna, clean your cell out, you're being upgraded. Come on, look lively now, I haven't got all day! Don't you want to move to a nice clean cell with a window and a light? Grown attached to this shithole, have you? Move!"

Natasha didn't know whether to believe her ears, nobody had spoken to her for ages. She didn't know whether she could trust this man, she knew only too well how much the guards liked to relieve their boredom by raising the hopes of the prisoners only to dash them again, and walk away laughing loudly. As she washed her cell out she kept recounting her system. She was sure she was right, her cell wasn't due a cleaning for another three body counts and four meals.

"Right, you do look a mess, you really do. I've seen better looking sixty-year-old scrubbers on the quayside. I wouldn't give you ten kopecks for a blowjob. Come on, outside with you. Don't forget your luggage!" She picked up her clean bucket. "Not that, stupid! Take your tray and your bowl with you!". She was walked up the corridor to her left between two guards, her eyes hurting especially when they approached one of the unshielded hundred-Watt bulbs hanging from the ceiling every fifteen yards.

Suddenly, they rounded a corner and it seemed as if Spring had arrived. She could see into the cells and those on the left had tiny windows high up in the wall. You'd need to be eight feet tall to see out of them, if they had been clean enough, but they did give the otherwise drab, bare cells a look of almost elegance, compared with where she had just come from.

They stopped outside an empty cell and she was encouraged to enter it. "Why am I being moved here?" she asked.

"Oh, not to her ladyship's liking, is it? Oh deary, deary me! What shall we do about that, Alexei? Get in and shut up or you'll go back to solitary".

They locked the railing behind themselves and walked off laughing about something that she thought she must have missed. She looked around, admiring the amount of space and light she had, and feeling stupid for doing so at the same time. The cell was tiny, eight feet by six. She noticed a woman looking at her from across the corridor.

"Hello, my name is Natasha".

"Who cares? You won't be here long, not if you're on that side".

"Do you know what day it is?"

"Who cares, time and date means nothing here?"

"Please?"

"It could be August 14th.

Natasha burst out laughing, "Oh, that's rich, that is! I can't believe it!"

"What's the matter? Gone stir crazy, have you? Couldn't take the solitary? You were only in there a while".

"Today is my twenty-sixth birthday!"

"It could be the thirteenth, or even the fifteenth of August…"

"I'll settle for the fourteenth," she replied, then she laid down on the thin straw mattress and slept. She dreamt she was at a children's birthday party and all her old school friends were there. Her father was bringing in bowls of food, laughing and joking with the children, but her mother was sitting in the corner scowling at her.

∞

When she awoke it was only because a guard was rattling her cage waiting to dispense food. She noted that she hadn't felt better for more than a month.

"Natalya Petrovna, you look a bloody mess. Hasn't anyone told you you need a shower?"

"No, comrade, nobody has said anything to me", she replied startled by the use of her name, the sudden interest in her appearance and the improvement in quality of the food.

"Sandr, report this oversight at once!" at which one of the guards hurried off, and the 'head' guard and the cook with the trolley moved on to the next cell out of sight.

Shortly after finishing her meal, which was really quite appetising compared to what she had been getting, a female guard appeared outside her cell. She opened it, slid back the gate and said, "Come with me, you need to get cleaned up".

They walked a short distance and the guard pointed into a dark room with no door. She flicked a switch and harsh yellow tube lights protected by thick glass covers burst into light.

"Strip off and shower".

As Natasha turned to face the guard she saw herself in a large metal mirror on the wall. The image that she beheld shocked her. She knew that her hair was bad, and she knew that her clothes were filthy, but her once-beautiful face and gorgeous eyes had been replaced by tight grey skin and sunken pits. She looked like one of the walking dead.

"Natalya Petrovna! I don't have all evening, strip and shower. You can throw those filthy rags in that bin and put these overalls on. The thought of clean clothes, even overalls, seemed too good to be true. The guard had to turn the water off after ten minutes because if the decision had been left to Natasha, she would have stayed there an hour even if the water was cold.

"Overalls on! Right, back to your cell". When they were inside, the guard asked for her measurements and made notes, then she locked the gate and left. Natasha dared to hope that she was about to be released, wasn't that what the old woman had meant earlier, she wondered?.

She couldn't say that it was the best birthday she'd ever had, but in a strange way it was. She was happier than she had been for several weeks and there seemed to be light at the end of the tunnel. She tried to think about her mother and wish her well. She knew that her mother had been held there, possibly even in that very cell, because she had heard Andropov order her detention, but she hadn't seen her on her two little walks that day.

She went back to sleep feeling clean and full and optimistic.

The following day, she received equally good treatment, and on the day after that too along with a bundle of cheap, but colourful clothing that actually looked as if it had been chosen with care, and a hair brush, lipstick and mascara.

"Don't wear the make-up in here", she was warned by the female guard who had been being nice to her for the last few days, "some of the animals that work in here don't get close to a pretty young lady very often... some never do".

It all sounded to Natasha as if she was getting out and even the Asian in her allowed her exuberance and hope to show on her face, when she knew that no-one could see.

On August 18th, she was awoken an hour early, fed, taken to the shower and told to make herself look as if she were going on a hot date. It was a tall order, but Natasha did her best and made a pretty good job of it. The extra food and extra hope had gone a long way to restoring her beauty and the make-up did most of the rest.

"Natalya Petrovna! Time to leave", shouted a male guard outside her cell as he unlocked the sliding gate. She walked out with a suppressed smile on her face. She put a thumb up to the old woman opposite, who gave no reaction, but to turn her back on her.

Two guards led her outside into the open air for the first time in more than a month and she sniffed the air as if it was the finest rose.

"Get in, you'll have plenty of time for poncing about smelling the air later".

"Where are we going?" she asked getting into the car.

"You'll find out soon enough, stop asking questions".

They pulled up at the Supreme Court and Natasha's heart sank. She had always known that a trial was going to be the next step, but she had allowed herself, foolishly, to believe that she might yet be pardoned. Perhaps that was going to happen now, she thought, but she didn't believe it any more. They took her in through a side entrance, signed her over to the police guards and they put her in a cell to await her turn.

It didn't take long, shortly after it had chimed ten thirty on a large clock outside the building, a police officer opened the holding cell.

"This way, please, Miss", he asked politely and took her upstairs in a lift to the second floor.

They sat outside the courtroom and waited to be called. When Natasha was, she was led to the dock, sworn in, her identity checked, then the charges were read out and she was asked for her plea. She was accused of abuse of public funds, dereliction of duty, bringing the Motherland into disrepute, intent to defect and high treason.

"How do you plead?" asked the most senior of the three judges. She looked around and a man sitting at the table marked 'Advocate for the Defence', whom she had never met or even seen before that moment, stood up and said, "I have recommended that my client pleads guilty on all counts except high treason, Comrade. We have come to this conclusion in light of the overwhelming, indisputable evidence, much of which has been given or corroborated by the defendant's own mother". He pointed to a withered old woman sitting behind him with a wave of his hand. Marina did not look up.

Natasha was dumbstruck.

"How do you plead, Natalya Petrovna Myrskii?" He waited ten seconds or so and then continued. "In light of the evidence and the defendant's unwillingness to cooperate with this court, I suggest we take her silence as confirmation of her guilt". He brought his gavel down with a loud bang, and chatted for a few seconds with his fellow judges.

"It is the opinion of this court that the defendant be taken from here to a penal institution for corrective labour and that she remain there for a period of no less than five years. Take her down!"

There were muted sounds of approval from the public gallery, but she wasn't thinking about that. If she had allowed herself to admit that she would be going to trial, as Andropov had told her himself that she would be, she would have known that her mother would have to be at the preliminary hearing and the trial, but seeing her actually taking part for the prosecution was still heartbreaking and demoralising.

That was Natasha's fifteen minutes of fame, except that the show trial was not televised as far as she knew because she could see no cameras or crew. She was taken back down to the holding cells to await the fate of whoever else was unfortunate enough also to be on trial that day.

Twelve of them, including one other woman, were taken to a police station when the court closed. They were to remain there until the Gulag worked out who could be best used in which camps. It took twenty-four hours, but Natasha was later to wish that it had taken twenty-four months.

She and the other woman were to be taken to a 'camp of corrective labour', often also called a Gulag, but incorrectly, which was situated almost a hundred kilometres north of Moscow. They were told nothing else, but didn't have to be, that was already the most distressing news either of the women had ever had in their lives. Only Siberia could have been worse.

The two army guards who drove them to their camp, offered them food for sex halfway, although they had been given money to feed their charges anyway. They both refused and didn't get any food.

"We could shoot you, if you'd prefer", offered one of the guards with a big smile. Both women ignored him, but wished many times later that they had taken him up on his generous offer. Guards received a reward for shooting runaway prisoners, as long as they were shot in the back with their heads pointing away from the shooter, but that was easy to arrange.

The weather was good and the fields were green as they drove north, but neither of the women was under any illusion about the sort of place they were heading for. It was called a camp, yes, but that was the only similarity it would share with the holiday camps like Sochi on the seasides around Russia. Natasha had five years of it as well, not only two weeks.

She found it difficult to talk to the other woman although she seemed nice enough and she was probably just as terrified as Natasha was. It just all seemed irrelevant now. The chances of dying in a camp were six times higher than outside, so she might never see the outside world as a free woman again. Her life was effectively over. The degradation, humility, hunger and hard physical work that the inmates underwent was well-known all over the Soviet Union and when a friend went into the Gulag Archipelago, you never expected to see him or her again, for true equality of the sexes was operated in the camps and most women could not keep up.

When they were approaching the camp, the gun towers were the first objects that stood out against the skyline, then the lower, grey, monotonous, concrete administration buildings and the even lower wooden barrack blocks. Lastly, the electrified barbed-wire fence and the main gate became apparent.

"Your new home, ladies, you stupid zeks, and it serves you right. You turned us down, but you'll get it up every hole you've got in there and you'll be glad of it. I know you don't believe me now, but you give it six months or a year and you'll understand".

They signed their charges over and left, and the women were led to reception.

"Fill out these forms, girls", said the desk sergeant cheerfully. "Thank you", he said smiling when they were finished.

"Follow me", he ordered leading them to a room off the main hall. "Strip naked. I need to check you for contraband and prohibited items". The internal searches were intimate and protracted, but when he had satisfied himself in more ways than one, he gave them a smock each. "You will wear these from now on, put your clothes in these plastic bags, seal the bags and I will sign for them. You'll get them back when you've done your time".

That was expected to be never, but they would never get their clothes or possessions back anyway, it was impossible, because the best items would be sold in town within a week and the rest would be exchanged for favours with inmates. There was always a shortage of clothing, especially in winter and official usage was one smock per person per year, although they rarely lasted three months of hard labour.

After the sergeant had had his perks, he called two guards who led the terrified women to their prison block. There were no cells, and there were no beds just fifty inmates to a barrack and one hundred barracks. People tried to personalise a space in a barrack with whatever they could collect. Natasha curled up into a ball and wondered what had gone so wrong in her life. Big things had been expected of her all her studying days and she had come to believe that she would be happy, but here she was reduced to sleeping on the floor in one of the hundred and fifty or so worst places in the Soviet Union.

This was a relatively small camp and the labour was not the worst kind. People feared the mines, especially the salt mines of Siberia, but this camp was involved with mixed farming and Natasha was assigned to the kitchens. She didn't know it, but it was the only concession her mother had been able to wring out of Andropov, and that was only because of their previous liaison in the good old days when it looked as if Operation Youriko would catapult her into the top spot of the Alma Ata Communist Party, from where she might make it to the Central Committee, when Natasha became more proficient at her job.

However, that all seemed such a long time ago at that moment.

Andropov's Cuckoo

12 GULAG ARCHIPELAGO

The kitchen staff may have had the easiest jobs, but they had the longest hours. The following morning, Natasha's barrack was awoken at four am. It transpired that everybody in her hut was on the kitchen detail, she drew her legs up under herself and watched the ragged, sad-faced, scrawny women shuffle past her. She had slept nearest the door, and the woman who had arrived with her slept opposite, head to the wall, feet towards the centre of the room with a gap for people to walk through. It was the best place to have during the summer when a cool breeze blew in under the doors or they would be left open entirely, but the summers north of Moscow were short. In the winter, those who had been there the longest were glad of their places nearest to the pot-bellied wood-burning stove.

She was watching her room-mates walk through the central gap now. No-one looked at her, no-one took any notice. She tagged on the end of the detail. They first went to the latrines, which were two long low walls running the length of the room on either side. The method appeared to be to sit on the first wall, lean back and support yourself on the second wall. Water ran in a gully along the wall of the building and there were scoops hanging from strings. The stench was much worse than a neglected cow shed.

From there, the women shuffled into the adjoining room where the water continued to flow in the gullies through holes in the wall. They slipped their smocks off, put them on the top of the wall above the gully and ladled water over themselves. Natasha was horrified at the emaciation of her fellow inmates. She had seen stray dogs in better condition. There was no means of drying oneself. This whole process took no longer than twenty minutes then the group moved, without the need for direction from the two guards, to the kitchen.

The first jobs were to light the series of open fires and put what was left of the soup from the day before on to warm up for breakfast. It would be wrong to call them leftovers, because given the paltry amount of food that was given to each inmate, there would never have been anything left over, if it had been down to the prisoners.

Thirty minutes later, the inmates, mostly male, eagerly shuffled past a long, shuttered opening in one of the walls holding up the bowls that they had tied to their waists for the regulation ladleful of thin gruel at breakfast. If Natasha had thought that the kitchen staff had looked rough, they looked positively affluent, well-dressed and overfed compared with the others. What shocked her the most was the look of sheer hopelessness in their sad, sunken, lifeless eyes.

She heard a slap and a scream from behind her in the kitchen and watched in horror as the guards beat the other new girl with batons as she huddled on the floor trying to protect herself. She found out later that her 'crime' was to have tasted the soup to see if it would benefit from more salt. Apparently, stealing food, for so was it described, was the second most serious infringement in the camp, but it too could be punished by death, as could trying to escape. The punishment for attacking a guard, the third most serious crime, was left to the discretion of the guard. If he or she had had a bad day, or was just sadistic, it often meant being beaten to death.

They were lenient on Anna, the other latest arrival, because she was new and hadn't yet learned the rules. Natasha wanted to go to help Anna to a corner to recover, but she caught the look in a colleague's eyes and realised that it was not done. Eventually, one of the guards dragged her out of the way and dropped her in a corner. Another of the many rules, which, if broken, could get you between one and half a dozen or more thwacks with a guard's baton, was talking at work.

When breakfast had been served, the kitchen staff divided into two parties: one did the washing up and cleaning and the other went to the prisoners' vegetable plot to collect the raw materials for lunch. Then these were washed, but not peeled, they never threw anything edible away, chopped and put into the huge cauldrons to boil. There was no meat. At eleven o'clock a two-gallon pot of bones arrived and that was distributed evenly between the simmering cauldrons.

The bones had come from the guards' mess. They had their own kitchen and their own cooks from the local village, because they didn't trust the inmates not to try to poison them. They ate well, and probably stole whatever meat ration was allowed the prisoners by the government, but they did pass down whatever was left to be mixed into the soup, which the guards insisted be called by its official name of 'stew'.

At midday, half of the cauldrons were taken to the fields on the back of a truck. It was considered a privilege to be chosen for this detail because it meant a pleasant ride across country and an easy two hours. Ten people did this every day, while the others tended the prisoners' plot near the cookhouse. When the empty cauldrons came back, they were filled to half with stew from the remaining cauldrons and they were all topped up to full with water

This meant that lunch was the most nutritious meal of the day. Three quarters of this was served up with a morsel of bread at six or seven depending on the season's light and how long it took them to walk back to the camp. The bread was also cooked on the premised and the grain had to be crushed between grindstones by hand. It was mostly unleavened, although they were sometimes given yeast.

After the evening meal, most people went back to their barrack and slept, but the kitchen staff had to clean up again, and thin the stew down once more for the next day's breakfast.

And so it went on, day after day after laborious day. People didn't talk to each other often. Perhaps, they could on 'hard labour', as it was called, but in the kitchen, the zeks, the name the prisoners were called by themselves and the staff, could not and she spent fourteen to seventeen hours a day in there. People had nothing to say anyway, didn't care and were too tired.

Every day was the same for everybody. Everybody got injured or fell sick at some time or another, but there was no medical staff for the inmates. If it was serious, they died, otherwise they got better and there was no such thing as time off. Sometimes, an illness brought in from the village would sweep through the whole camp, spread by an infected guardhouse cook, but everyone was so weak that they had no resistance to disease or infection.

People died every week, it was just a question of how many and who. None of the inmates knew exactly: twenty to thirty in the summer and double that or more in the winter. It wasn't worth making friends with anyone, the chances were they wouldn't last long. Friends fell sick too like everyone else and then you had to try to help, except there was nothing you could do, so you had to feel sorry for them, but nobody had the energy for sympathy.

A new intake was usually fit for the first six months, but after that they just looked like everyone else, battered survivors from some war-torn, bomb-blasted city. The best strategy, the one universally adopted by the long-timers, was polite indifference. They kept themselves to themselves, looked after number one and concentrated on staying alive for just one more day.

Natasha witnessed a lot of needless violence by the guards against the prisoners. Some guards were more guilty than others by a long chalk, and the zeks were particularly obsequious to these, but they had to be careful, because that could make one of the 'nicer' guards jealous. Walking this thin line while suffering from exhaustion and malnutrition led to frayed nerves. It was another good reason why people didn't say much.

Sometimes, once or twice a week, a fight would break out between two inmates. Nobody ever helped anybody out, so it was invariably one to one. It was illegal for inmates to carry anything that could be conceived of as a weapon, but many prisoners did carry pieces of wood sharpened into stilettos. When a fight broke out, usually over something petty, the guards and prisoners alike would flock to watch.

The guards were supposed to break the fights up and punish the participants, but they always got there 'too late'. Often, they could be seen betting on the outcome, which was always the death of one or both of the combatants from stab wounds. It was the only entertainment that the camp provided, and it caused great excitement. People became animals, no, worse than animals, they wanted to see blood, and pain and death to work off some of their own resentment and anger.

The winner, if there was one, would be arrested, slung into solitary and put on half-rations, which was usually enough to kill him, or, rarely, her, from infected wounds and malnutrition within a week. Many realised too late that it was better to lose and die quickly, but those that survived the fight and the solitary were treated like royalty by the prisoners. People deferred to them and never argued with them, but there weren't many in that exalted upper class of inmates.

Ex-doctors came close, but the complete absence of medication reduced their normal success rate considerably. However they knew more than most, so to have a doctor as an acquaintance was seen as a definite advantage. The kitchen staff carried a certain amount of kudos too. Those on hard labour hoped at some point during their stay that making special friends with a woman that doled out the food could help, and it was true, it could.

There were no regulations about how many pieces of vegetable or bone a prisoner received with each meal, the only stipulation was the overall quantity: one ladle, one and a half, or, on rare occasions, two ladles. The guards watched carefully to ensure there was no favouritism, but a skilled ladler could ensure that a bowl received more pieces than usual, or even none. In fact, many people didn't get anything but stock, because the stew was so thin, especially at breakfast. This led to liaisons between warriors, doctors and cooks. Sex between prisoners was disallowed, but it went on, especially if a guard could watch or get his share first.

There was a lot more sexual activity between the guards and the prisoners though, homo- and heterosexual. Homosexuality was strictly forbidden in Soviet society, but who was there to complain to in the camps? Some men entered into these relationships willingly, others not so, and some for special privileges like bread or a cigarette. The women were the same, those that had been there a while openly offered sex for favours, the guards that had brought Natasha and Anna to the camp had been right.

Natasha was almost reduced to having to go down the same route when her smock became so threadbare and fragile, that she was already using thin twigs to hold it together in places. With no underwear, she would soon be naked. She had realised the problem, when she had to use the first twig on her right shoulder and had been searching for a solution for a couple of weeks, when, while working in the prisoners' sweet corn patch, she came across the lifeless body of a colleague from the kitchen.

She had pulled the woman's smock up and off and stripped her own off to switch them when she noticed another colleague watching. Natasha had felt ashamed, robbing a corpse, something she would never have dreamed of outside, but after a few seconds of staring into each other's eyes, Natasha had carried on dressing them both and the colleague had walked away. It was never mentioned, but Natasha knew that her 'new' dress only had a few months' wear in it and then what?

Doctors could get more clothes than most, she thought, because they saw more deaths. It was something to bear in mind, and she knew that she had to give it serious consideration. It was her best option and carried the added benefit of healthcare, such as it was.

Even after the very first month into her sentence, Natasha was beginning to lose weight and feel hungry. She had learned the official camp rules quite quickly without having to suffer a beating, although she had had one for 'being too slow'. It was an excuse, it had just been her turn. She had seen it before, but not realised what she was witnessing. A guard had had a bad day and wanted to take it out on someone. When this happened, the other guard in the cookhouse usually watched or joined in.

When Natasha was being beaten she noticed several of the old lags taking the opportunity to steal a mouthful of soup. They never took bread because they might get caught trying to chew or swallow it, but soup went down quickly. She learned other ruses too, such as drinking the washing up water. They didn't use a cleaning agent, so the greasy water always contained some calories and even the odd shred of vegetable, but never any bones. The bones were highly sought after, since they were the only source of calcium on the camp available to the prisoners, unless you did what a lot did.

Eat bugs.

Insects were a useful source of calcium and protein. All the long-timers ate them. They ate worms too, and snails and snakes and rats. Snakes and rats were rare luxuries, but insects, worms and snails could be collected from the fields and roasted in a pan over an open fire. Most beetles could be fried in a dry pan and their bodies would give off enough fat to cook the worms and snails in. Otherwise, the latter had to be boiled, but they weren't so palatable then. The easiest insects to catch were cockroaches, but they were the least tasty and were only to be found in the latrines, because there was no other source of food for them – the humans had already picked it clean.

Some gourmets only used cockroaches to drain their oil for cooking more delicious morsels, then they would trade the cooked cockroaches with other zecs, sometimes for sex and sometimes for clothing liberated from one of the fallen.

Natasha managed to stay in pretty good shape by stealing mouthfuls of soup, drinking washing-up water and eating insects, but this also had its drawbacks. She was already one of the youngest women on the camp and she was one of the newest for a while, and they were always in demand, but she was just about the best looking too, because she had kept most of her figure. Most of the other women had lost their breasts months or years ago, melted down by their bodies to nourish more vital parts.

One trick she employed was to tie a strip of cloth tight around her breasts so that she looked flat-chested, but it didn't help a lot. She, like all the younger women, was molested and raped from time to time. It became just another one of those things, like being hungry or tired. She often wondered why she didn't become pregnant. Some women did, but most didn't. Perhaps it was due to malnourishment, she thought. Those babies who were born on the camp and didn't die, were taken away to orphanages.

Anna, the only person she knew who wanted nothing but friendship from her, often said that she could take the beatings, the rapes and the general humiliation no longer. She had been low for weeks, but some had been depressed for years, it was not unusual.

"Come on, Anna, we've done two years, we can do this together", she said while in the latrine one morning. "You got five years too, so in six months we'll have done half of it, and then it's all down hill. We'll walk out of here together".

"I value your friendship, Natasha, but I miss my two little boys so much… I even miss my drunken old husband, though I never thought I'd say that. I just want to get back to my family. This, all this, is just so, so vile, so inhuman. No sane human being could make other people go through what we have to put up with… and for what? Some of us don't even know why we're here.

"I read some samizdat literature, so what? Five years for reading some banned books? That is just not sane".

Natasha had hugged her and felt her sob, but a guard had shouted at them from outside the door to stop.

"We're not even allowed to console each other! I don't know how much more I can take, Nat, I really don't".

"Please don't talk like that, Anna, you're scaring me. You are the only person I care about for thousands of miles, and if I didn't have you, I don't know what I'd do. You give me strength. Come on, we'd better get out of here before that bitch takes to us, she's looking over again".

One afternoon two days later, while working in the prisoners' plot, Anna doused herself in water, started singing and jumped onto the electrified fence. As she hung on the barbed-wire, smouldering a little, two guards used her for target practice in the hope of getting a reward.

She was left there for more than ten minutes while a guard walked to the office to have the electricity turned off, it was sickening and many people wretched at the smell and the horror, but they had nothing inside them to bring up. Natasha raged and shouted at the guards until one of them raised his rifle to her. She held up her hands and stood still. She knew better than to turn her back on them, because then they could claim she was trying to run away and shoot her. They would even get a reward for it, and although she was in the mood to die, she didn't want any guards to profit from her death.

There was no funeral for Anna, but then there never was for prisoners, they were just thrown in a hole in one of the fields with any other rubbish that was of no use and covered over. There was no ceremony, no farewells. Most people thought she had been brave and envied her her courage, but Anna's death had a profound effect on Natasha, she was seriously thinking of taking her friend's route to freedom.

A few days later, a guard laid her baton on Natasha's shoulder while she was checking a pot of stew, she consciously relaxed knowing that that was the best way to avoid broken bones in the beating that would surely follow. She had been expecting some sort of retaliation for her outburst over Anna's death.

"Outside, you! The commandant wants to see you. On the double!"

Natasha did what passed for a trot among the exhausted inmates and went outside where she was met by an armed escort and taken away. It was usually bad news to come to the attention of the commandant. Natasha had been on her knees before him several times, but that had always been in the evening when no-one else was about to bear witness.. She still thought it had to be about her outburst over the treatment of Anna's dead body. Someone would have put that in a report.

She was not kept in suspense for long.

"Ah, 4626346 Myrskii. You were sentenced to five years… for Oh! Quite a list of things, but the charge of treason was dropped I see…"

That was news to Natasha, no-one had told her. She just stood up straight and stared forward.

"You have only served two years and one month of that sentence… Well, I received a very unusual letter yesterday, so unusual that I asked for the verification of its contents, but it is correct. You are to be released into the custody of the Moscow City Police Force immediately. They have not arrived yet, but they should be here within the hour.

"Congratulations, you seem to have some powerful friends. Go and get your things, have a shower and smarten yourself up, you look like a rag doll. That is all, you may wait outside when you are ready".

"Get her some decent clothes to wear, even if they don't fit", he shouted to his secretary.

Natasha had to be led outside. She couldn't believe what had just happened. It made no sense… no-one got out of a corrective labour camp early, most didn't even get out on time. She hurried over for a shower and someone left a bundle of clothes for her to wear. She put them on and tucked her smock behind the bench knowing that someone would find it and be grateful. She had nothing to collect, that had been a sick joke.

She crossed the yard to the administration block and sat on a bench outside to await the police car. She looked like a schoolgirl dressed in her father's clothes but she felt on top of the world. She didn't waste any time wondering who had gotten her out or what they had in mind for her. She would do anything and everything to stay out of the camps. She had been in one of the easier ones, but it still had been worse than any Hell she could ever have imagined.

Andropov's Cuckoo

13 A NEW JOB

Natasha had been taken back to the same police station that she had been held in two years before, and it could even have been the same holding cell for all she could remember, but it was like a luxury hotel to her this time. She fancied that it had just been redecorated, or maybe it was just her acute sense of smell. She was given better food than she had had for years and she didn't even have to cook it herself. Lights went out at nine o'clock and she slept like a baby. It was the best night's sleep she'd had as far back as she could remember, certainly before she had moved to Tokyo.

She was awoken for breakfast at eight, told to shower and led outside to a police car. She didn't ask where they were taking her, she didn't care, as long as it wasn't up north again and she was only mildly surprised when the car stopped outside the Lubyanka, but very thankful when she was taken up to the third floor, not to the cells.

When the green light came on, she was shown into Andropov's office.

"Ah", he said when they were alone, "it is little Comrade Natasha, or is it Yui or Aki? My Little Cuckoo… Who are you today? Where did you get those clothes? They look quite fetching in a strange waifish sort of a way… Please take a seat".

"I will be whoever you want me to be, Comrade Andropov".

"Good answer, comrade, you are learning. Did you learn that in our little camp of correction?"

"I learned many things in that camp, Comrade Andropov".

"Did you learn that you never want to go back their again? That you would do anything, anything in the world, never to have to go back there again, comrade?"

"Yes, I did, comrade".

"Good. Excellent! So, if I were to find you little jobs to do, you would be happy to oblige me?"

"Yes, comrade, of course, anything".

"Fine, I suppose you are wondering how you got out early, aren't you? Have you spoken to your mother recently?"

"Not for more than two years, comrade".

"No, I suppose not… Anyway, she is at death's door, so she tells me," he held up a letter and waved it about. "She implored me to help you as her dying wish… in fact she has written to me many times on the subject. Anyway, we got to be quite close friends, your mother and I, when we were setting up Operation Youriko, so in the light of that I ordered your conditional release. It quite upset the camp commandant apparently… He asked for confirmation of my orders! Cheeky blighter, still not many are released before they complete their sentence, so I suppose I can't blame him, eh?" Natasha said nothing but put on the tiniest of smiles.

I don't suppose you know this, but I used to find the notes you made in Bonn about some of the diplomats highly amusing. You see, I know or have met nearly everyone you reported on… It made it difficult to keep a straight face when I met some of them again. It really was very funny to think of that pompous ass French Under Secretary stroking a hostess' bottom in public when he'd had too much to drink and he thought his wife wasn't watching!

"I wish I'd been there… The next time I saw him was in Sweden and when a, shall we say, shapely woman bent over before us, I looked him in the eyes and then down at her derrière and raised my eyebrows. He pretended that butter wouldn't melt in his mouth, but I thought 'You lecherous old hypocrite'.

"Yes, I've had some fun with your observations and we were, still are, in fact, putting them to good use, which is another reason why I ordered your release, when your mother pleaded for it again. I have always had a soft spot for you, as I have said before, but that didn't mean you could go unpunished… No, quite the contrary. However, that is all behind us now.

"I have a proposition to put to you, not much of a choice really, it's either accept it or go back to finish your sentence. Anyway, we have a fledgling strategy, actually, most countries employ it, and I want you to take part in it for us. A fledgling strategy for a Little Cuckoo… that's really quite good, isn't it? Nevertheless, we would like to see this strategy developed more inside the Motherland and I think that you're the right girl to do it. What do you say?"

"I say, 'Yes of course I will', comrade".

"All right, good girl, but you are not looking your best at the moment. We will need to remedy that first, the job requires you to be in the peak of health. There is a sanatorium, no, that is not what they call them these days, what does my wife say? Ah, 'health spa', that's it. There is a health spa that some of the wives use to get into tip-top condition. I want you to go there and come out looking like you did before.

"How about clothes? You can't go about dressed like that".

"Only what you see, comrade".

"Well, they are quite fetching in a tom-boyish kind of way, but not at all suitable. Do you have any money?"

"No, sir, not a kopeck".

"All right", he said reaching into a draw, "here is your old bank book from Alma Ata, and I'll have the money you earned as Yui transferred into it today. Stay at the Moskovskaya Hotel and I'll have someone contact you about the health spa. I want you to go there tomorrow, it's not far. The quicker you get into shape, the sooner we can get you back to work.

"Well, it has been nice to see you again, Comrade Natalya Petrovna, we'll say 'Goodbye' for now".

"Goodbye, Comrade Andropov, and thank you for giving me a second chance".

"Thank your mother, but if you screw up on this job, you will die in a salt mine in Siberia and you can take that as my solemn oath. You really upset me last time, I took it quite personally".

They released her onto the square outside without any money, but she didn't care, she was free! She walked around aimlessly until she stumbled upon a bank, then she withdrew a thousand roubles and took a taxi to the Red Square, where she bought five hundred roubles worth of new clothes and a suitcase. She put the prettiest outfit on and stored the rest in the case, including the prison outfit which she wanted to keep as a souvenir, then she booked into the nearby Moskovskaya, put her things in her room and went down to the hotel restaurant.

"Please tell reception that Natalya Petrovna Myrskii of room 511 is in the restaurant if anyone comes. I am expecting visitors", she said to the barman as she perched upon a stool, "but before you do that, will you pour me the biggest and coldest glass of Urquell Pilsner beer you have. I am dying of thirst".

She had a slap-up meal, two bottles of Urquell and then went to her room where she threw up in the toilet, had a shower and went to sleep on the bed in jeans and a T-shirt for want of any night things or a dressing gown. Some time in the late afternoon, she was awoken by a knock on the door, and with her five o'clock hangover, it took her a moment to remember where she was.

"Come in!" she called and then realised that she had locked the only door she had had control over for more than two years. "Coming!" she shouted.

"Good afternoon, Comrade Natalya Petrovna?" asked the middle-aged, but fit, office-type woman, "May I come in?" Natasha stepped aside to allow her access.

"Take a seat, er...?" she said pointing at the table by the window looking out over St Basil's Cathedral.

"Olga Andreyevna. What a lovely view, isn't it? One of the best in Moscow, I'd say. Now, down to business. You are joining our fitness programme tomorrow at the Yuri Gagarin Health Spa, is that correct?"

"Yes, it has been recommended to me".

"Yes, so I see. Well, I don't have a lot to add to what's in the brochures, this envelope is for you. Inside, you have directions, your entry pass and voucher and our brochure. If you don't have any of the kit you need, it can be purchased there. What time will you be arriving, Comrade Natalya Petrovna?"

"When do you want me, I'm easy?"

"We are running a heath spa, not a prison camp, you know?" she joked, "you can arrive when you like. Check out is before eleven and check in after midday. You are booked in and paid for, full board, for two weeks. I hope to see you again. That's it, Comrade Natalya Petrovna, I'll be on my way now".

"See you there and thank you".

Natasha had another shower, a warm one, and went back to the restaurant to try again.

∞

At the health spa, early the next afternoon, she found that she was sharing the room with a woman of about her own age. Apparently, the reason was because people were less likely to cheat – eat or drink extra – if they could get caught. It seemed odd to Natasha, because she was there to put weight on, and her room-mate didn't look overweight either. Still, everything that wasn't being in the camp was a bonus, so she just accepted it.

Natasha soon realised that there were several programmes at the spa. Her wing of the large country building was female only, but within it, there were courses for recovering alcoholics, recovering anorexics, weight loss, cosmetics, massage, T'ai Chi and several others. Some people, like Natasha and her room-mate, Irina, were booked onto several courses including weight normalisation, cosmetics, massage and T'ai Chi.

Their programmes lasted until tea time, when the last meal of the day was served. They were not allowed to leave the grounds or visit the male wing, but were encouraged to swim, play cards, watch television in the communal lounge or otherwise socialise until lights out at nine. No alcohol was allowed. On the third evening, Natasha, Irina and ten other young women were instructed to attend a special lecture.

"Some of you will already know why you are here, others will not. I will explain. You have been selected or you have volunteered for this work, I will not go any further into that subject, you know who you are. What I am about to say may not be repeated... ever. The government has recognised a need to stay ahead in the ever-increasingly complicated world of espionage. Bugging has been successful for the last few decades, but as technology has become more powerful, so have the methods of detecting it. Nowadays, you can put a bug in an office and they will find it the same day. When I say, 'they' I mean 'us' too. Although we are only trying to match the capitalists at their game, we are necessarily involved as well.

"We did not start this, we are just trying to keep a level playing field. So, since technological methods fail so regularly, we are initiating a programme of personnel who are willing to be the listening devices. Do not be alarmed, we are not going to insert bugs under your skin... We want you to be the eyes and ears of the state. This will involve close personal contact with the enemy, but it is not dangerous work, because you will always be operating on Soviet soil, and, I might add, usually on some of its best soil. Moscow, Leningrad,

Kalinin, The Black Sea, like Sochi and many other resorts on the coast and inland.

"You will earn your salaries by watching, listening, and reporting. You all speak foreign languages and you will be mostly working with foreign visitors, so you will often be in the best hotels, the best restaurants and the best bars. However, you may be directed at specific Soviet targets from time to time as well. That will be up to your controller.

"We propose to establish two teams of girls. You, Comrade Natalya Petrovna will lead one and you Comrade Irina Mikhailovna will lead the other. In order to help you put your targets more at ease, you will learn certain techniques for relaxing men at this spa. Now, I realise that all you beautiful young women probably already have a good idea what men like, but we will be teaching you advanced cosmetic techniques and basic T'ai Chi and massage. Men love to feel a woman's fingers massaging oil into their bodies and can't resist watching a woman stretching in her leotard.

"We will be teaching you these techniques. We also have some required reading. Please collect a book from each pile on your way out. I will contact you again tomorrow, goodbye for now".

"I've never heard of Mata Hari," said Irina lying on her bed, thumbing through the first of the books.

"Wait till you see what's in the other one…" said Natasha.

"Er, 'The Kama Sutra'? Never heard of that one either… Oh, my God! It looks interesting though. I should be able to learn this one, or I won't mind trying… however long it takes…"

When they had finished their courses at the health spa, the twelve women were ensconced in six double rooms in the Moskovskaya Hotel, where they worked with the serving staff some days, and learned polite eating habits and table etiquette from dedicated teachers for another fortnight. Natasha and some of the others already knew how Westerners expected people to behave at a table, but their were others for whom the course was very instructive and surprising.

Natasha didn't see Andropov again, dealing only with her controller. This team set-up suited her a lot better. She could play Agony Aunt by talking to her girls and discussing their mutual problems, and seek advice from a superior if she didn't have the answers herself. It was exactly what she had wanted in her previous life as Yui.

"This is a new concept in domestic surveillance for us in the Soviet Union, Comrades Natalya and Irina", repeated the chief controller the Saturday afternoon following the end of the course in the hotel. "Other countries have been operating such systems for many years, but this is new venture for us, and you and your teams are at the very forefront. The spearhead, so to speak. You should encourage your team members to cement lasting relationships with the men they meet. The secret of this type of work is going deep. You are not looking for a dinner, a dance, a kiss and cuddle. You want a deep, long-standing relationship where he will trust you and open his heart to you. Do you understand, comrades?"

They both nodded.

About half of the men you will meet will already have good jobs, but the others may be students who may have top positions in the future. We will run background checks as far as we can and try to point you in the right direction.

"Is there anything you'd like to ask us, comrades?"

Irina shook her head, "No, comrade, everything is quite clear'.

"Good! Comrade Natalya?"

"There is just one thing. I will keep my official name as it is, but I would like my operational name to be Youriko".

"Youriko? Just Youriko? Would you spell that for me, please? Why Youriko, might I ask?"

"I owe it to a few people", she explained after spelling the name.

"Just Youriko, no patronymic or surname?"

"No, just Youriko, it is enough, thank you".

"The records shall be so amended. Now, finally, here are envelopes with your instructors on where to go, where to stay etc and suggestions on where to go hunting. If you are not given a specific name, just go for foreigners. This first operation is a trial run, so you are both staying close to home. Irina, you will be working on foreign students visiting or studying in Moscow, and Nat…, er, I mean, er, Youriko, you will be taking your team to Kalinin also to work on foreign students. They should be easy meat for a bunch of beautiful women like you and your teams.

"So, good luck and good hunting and for the love of the Motherland, keep in touch!"

The three controllers shook hands with Irina and Natasha, but the latter two also kissed each other on the cheek, "Good luck, sister", said Natasha.

"You too, sister," repeated Irina, surprised by the informality, but touched by it as well.

That evening, Natasha read her sealed instructions, which were a lot more blatant than anybody had put them so far, although everyone knew how far they were expected to go achieve their goals. So, Natasha called the girls in the other two rooms and suggested going out for a drink and a meal, as they would be leaving for their first port of call the next day.

The 'work's do' was up beat and everyone had a good time. Natasha knew that she had a great team of good-time girls and that they were going to have a ball.

Kalinin was a fairly large university city that had become practically a suburb of Moscow. During Russian term-time it was filled with thousands of earnest young Soviet students, but when they went to work on the land or in the factories as part of the Komsomol or Communist Youth programme in the summer recess, the university earned extra foreign currency, called valuta, by teaching Russian language and Soviet history to foreign students. They also did short courses between terms.

There were four hundred British university students there and some of their teachers when Youriko's team of six stunners arrived. They checked into their assigned guest house and went for a look around posing as six university friends from Leningrad on holiday. It was a Sunday afternoon when they arrived, so there were no lessons, and the bars were full of Brits letting off steam. It was just the atmosphere the girls were looking for. So, they bought a pint of beer and a shot of vodka each and sat at a table giving the boys the eye and their best giggling smiles. It wasn't long before they were all bending over way further than they needed to play Russian billiards and accepting advice on how to play from people who knew the game far less well than they did themselves.

By closing time, all the girls had names and hotel room numbers from hopeful young men, and two of her girls went off with two men in search of a restaurant that someone said might still be open. She had advised them to stay in pairs if they could in the beginning and she was glad to see that they were listening to her. At twenty-eight, she was the eldest in the group by three years and she felt responsible for them. They all spoke English fluently, and some spoke other languages as well, but none of them had ever been abroad or had contact with Western foreigners, not that Natasha considered them at all dangerous.

Natasha was also five years older than most of the students she met, but they didn't know how to read her oriental features or her petite build, so she found it easy to get away with being twenty-two. She had given her student a French kiss and promised to meet him in the same bar after lessons at four thirty the next day. So had all the others.

It was like shooting fish in a barrel. In their early twenties, the students were all sex-mad and desperate to be one of the ones who 'slept with a Russian bird'. When the team's six weeks in Kalinin were up they had all been through several students and a couple of teachers each. They had names, addresses and phone numbers in the UK and promises to write. Most of the girls had received gifts in sterling or dollars and Natasha had got a teacher to promise to send her £100 a month 'to help her support her sick mother'.

She wasn't even sure whether she had a sick mother any longer or a mother at all. However, what was more important to the controller were the compromising photographs and audio tapes. The girls would insist on making love with the windows open or in the fresh air, where photographers waited to snap them as tape recorders in their bags or microphones hidden in the room's radios recorded the girls screaming and grunting in ecstasy. The boys loved hearing the noises, but little did they know that it was in anticipation of their bonuses, not the next thrust.

Natasha's controller congratulated her on a very successful first operation and in the New Year, sent her and her team off to Leningrad for a year. The girls were very excited to be going to Russia's most beautiful city and couldn't wait to meet a new batch of young men.

Andropov's Cuckoo

14 LENINGRAD 1978

Natasha loved Leningrad, but then so did everyone else. Moscow was the serious city of business and politics, large, grey, solid and domineering, but Leningrad was the opposite, more fun, light-hearted and open-planned. Moscow was old, at least nine hundred years old, but Leningrad was young, barely a third of that. She and her team went from success to success in their quest for making contacts among foreign visitors, obtaining their personal and business or college details and audio-visual evidence of compromising assignations.

They didn't uncover big secrets, but they helped to build profiles of young people, especially men, but also some women, who might come in useful in the future. As her controller kept saying to her, 'Today's bright young, drunken students will be tomorrow's politicians and captains of industry'. She was practising with several cover stories and personas, but she had to be careful not to overstep any marks, even ones she hadn't been told about, so she checked everything with her superiors first. She was well aware that this was her last chance.

"I have been told to tell you, Natasha, that as Youriko you may claim to be whoever you please. You can say you're Kazakh, Russian or Japanese. You may also be a student, or employed, in any nationality, just don't tell anyone your true purpose because it would defeat the object".

"Thank you, comrade, I would never disclose our operation to anyone, I can promise you that. Were you able to get me a Japanese passport or identity card to complete the disguise?"

"I have been told that they will supply you with a document that will pass for a Japanese identity card, but which will not stand up to scrutiny by the Japanese authorities. It will arrive in about two weeks".

He obviously hadn't known where she had worked and that she would have spotted that, but she didn't mention it.

She liked to say that she worked at the Japanese Embassy in Moscow, or Bonn and was on holiday in Leningrad for a month. It gave her more status with the businessmen who outnumbered the students except in the summer months and were more her age group. They also had more to offer in the short term. Claiming to be Japanese also threw people off their guard. Foreigners were naturally wary of Russians, because they could be up to any tricks, which she was, but being Japanese made her an ally automatically. It made it easier to win people's trust.

She went out with a businessman from Chicago, who told her that the auto-engineering firm he worked for was developing a brand new fuel injection system, which would revolutionise the internal combustion engine. She stayed with him for the two weeks of his trip and passed on details of the company, the main personnel, the chief designer, and the device itself, although it was not a subject she knew anything about.

However, that was not important. The information would be studied by experts who did understand and the company would be investigated, and then, if it was thought to be worthwhile, the company could be bought, or broken into, or the businessman blackmailed to get more details or perhaps the chief designer could be encouraged to betray his employers. She didn't know what would happen next and didn't really care, it was out of her hands and none of her business. She only had one goal – to stay out of the camps, and the only way she had of doing that was by pleasing her masters. If people trusted her too easily or talked too much that was their own lookout. She had problems enough of her own.

He was history now. She already had her sights on a journalist who was covering a peace conference in Leningrad. She had been told where he was staying and where he liked to drink and eat, so she just had to be there and get noticed, which she found she could do easily. She had never been all that interested in men before, but she found the company better than loneliness, and Leningrad better than the alternative.

In fact, Natasha quite enjoyed her new job, and she was starting to become well-known around the hotels, bars and restaurants where foreigners went. She often thought she recognised a knowing look in the eyes of a barman or maître d'hôtel many of whom were also informants for the KGB, especially in the valuta bars – bars where only foreign currency could be used and Russians were not allowed to go. If they suspected that she was really Soviet, then they would have reported her, but since no action had been taken against her, they were obviously surmising that she was an informer too - one of them and hence the unexpected smile or knowing look.

It amused her to consider that they may even have thought her to be a fully-fledged KGB officer, after all, she was paying in valuta sometimes and she did have her Japanese ID, which, she had had to show now and then. Her!? KGB!? It really was a rib-tickler! If only they knew anything about her! Suddenly, it occurred to her for the first time that her mother had probably been KGB, if she wasn't still.

One afternoon, while she was sitting in the underground valuta bar of the Evropeyskaya Hotel with two of her colleagues, just passing time drinking coffee, hoping that something interesting would happen, she idly watched two young men walk in, buy vodkas and tonic and take a seat a few tables away.

"Youriko, are you listening to me?"

"No, sorry, I was miles away, thinking about my mother. What is it?"

"Never mind, I thought you were listening I'm not going through all that again", and she carried on talking to her friend.

"How did you know about this place, Will? Have you been here before?" asked Tom, one of the two young men.

"No, I told you. I came to Leningrad for a day on a school cruise. We had high tea upstairs in the restaurant, but I got bored and walked around the hotel, until I found myself in here and they escorted me back to my party".

"But you said you were only fourteen when you came here last time… how did you…"

"I don't know, Tom, it's funny the things you remember, isn't it?"

"Well, I don't know, Will, but to remember a bar from ten years ago when you didn't even use to drink, that's bloody incredible".

"It's not incredible, is it? I got you here".

"Yep, well, I can't argue with that, me ol' mate. Cheers! Say, who are those girls down there? Don't say they remember you from back then as well?"

"Very funny! How am I supposed to know who they are? I just walked in here with you five minutes ago. They look like Japanese tourists to me… they can't be Russian or they wouldn't be in here".

"I don't know, but that one has been staring at you ever since we walked in. I've been watching her watching you. I noticed her watching you first in the mirror behind the bar when you were ordering the drinks. Very quiet in here, isn't it? There're only five of us and a barman".

"It says over there: 'Open from Four till Midnight'. It's only four thirty now, Tom. We can finish this and move on if you like".

"No, I'm all right, I don't mind quiet when the scenery is so beautiful. Why don't you ask if we can buy them a drink? Go on, it's my round".

"Well, why don't you ask them then?"

"No, that one fancies you, you ask her… You'll stand more chance".

"In what language?"

"You don't speak Japanese as well, do you? Blimey!"

"Of course I don't, I meant English or Russian, you dope!"

"Oh, aye, er, well if they're tourists they might not speak Russian, so you'd better try English, eh?".

"OK, here goes. Wish me luck", said Will getting up and approaching the girls' table. "Excuse me, ladies, do you speak English?"

"Yes, a little", replied Youriko.

"My friend and I have just arrived in Russia and we don't know anybody, so we wondered if we could buy you a drink and pick your brains".

"Sure", replied Youriko, pulling the seat next to her out, "please sit down".

Will called Tom over, the introductions were made and they sat down.

"When did you arrive?" asked Youriko.

"About an hour ago", answered Will, "well, touch down was about three hours ago, but we didn't get to the Leningradskaya Hotel until about an hour ago".

"Oh, you are staying there, are you? It is very nice… New and modern. Are you students, coming here to learn Russian?".

"Yes, we've got six weeks. How about you?"

"We, Aki and I, are exchange students from Japan. We are studying in Alma Ata university with our friend here Erna, and she has brought us to Leningrad for the summer holiday".

It became obvious very quickly that Will and Youriko had hit it off and that Tom was interested in Aki. Erna looked bored, but she stayed for a few free rounds then mumbled something unintelligible to Youriko, said 'Goodbye' to the two men and left.

"What language was that?" asked Tom.

"Kazakh", replied Aki looking at her friend with a shrug.

"Yes, we're picking it while in university down there", explained Youriko.

They spent the whole evening talking and drinking, until Youriko surprised the men by announcing that they had to go.

"Yes, sorry to split up the party, but it's eleven thirty and I must do something tomorrow".

"Oh, OK", said Will terribly disappointed, "do you live far from here?"

"No, just over the river".

"Can we walk you home then?" asked Tom. "Do you both stay together?"

"Yes, we have rented a small house. You may walk us home if you like. Thank you, but we must hurry".

They walked in couples over the nearest bridge and then a hooter sounded. "Watch this", said Aki, "many people come to see it every night".

The bridge cracked in the middle and both halves of the road started to raise. When they were fully up, the ships below, which Will had assumed were moored up, passed through.

"People come to see this every night", said Youriko proudly, "it is a big tourist attraction at every bridge on the Neva in Leningrad. It is very beautiful, no? With the old architecture, the moon on the water... Oh, I love Leningrad, it is so romantic".

The other three agreed enthusiastically and they resumed their walk to the girls' home, where they stood outside the front door and said 'Goodnight'.

"Which is the best way to get back to the Leningradskaya, Youriko?" asked Will.

"Oh, yes! You live on the other side... you can't get back until six o'clock! I am sorry, I didn't think. How stupid of me! I was having such a good time that I completely forgot that you are living on that side".

"Can't we get a taxi and go up or down river to cross?" asked Tom.

"No, Tom, there is no way... except, er..."

"What?" asked Will.

"To swim!" and Youriko and Aki laughed.

"Very good," said Will wondering if the girls had done this on purpose in revenge for some transgression that they knew nothing about, but Youriko later admitted that she had been enjoying herself so much that she hadn't thought about the bridges until it was too late.

"So what can we do now, Youriko?"

"You can sleep on the floor in our house", she replied looking at Aki for another suggestion, "but you must be very quiet and leave at five forty-five. We are not allowed male visitors and there are other girls asleep here. Come in quietly, no talking".

The girls collected pillows and blankets and made a makeshift bed up behind the sofa and left them to it.

"Great!" said Tom in a whisper. "First night in Russia, we pick up two birds go back to their house which is full of girls and you and I have to sleep together on the floor behind the couch. If you tell anyone, I'll kill you. Now goodnight!"

"Night, Tom".

They were awoken at five thirty by Youriko and Aki fully dressed bearing coffee and buttered toast. They were followed by the four other girls in their team over the next fifteen minutes in various states of undress. They had been warned that there were men in the living room but they wanted to see them for themselves and they had to pass through there to get to the kitchen and the bathroom anyway.

"Your taxi's here", announced one of the girls looking through the net curtain".

"Thanks for looking after us, Youriko", said Will., "Can I see you tonight?"

"Yes, if you want to… same time and place?"

"Yes," replied Will and Tom together. Will saw Tom lean over and kiss Aki, so he did the same to Youriko.

"Go on hurry", she chided, "See you later".

The taxi waiting outside beeped at five forty-five, Will and Tom rushed out to it, while the girls watched from behind the net curtains then it took them to the bridge where it joined the queue to cross over.

They arrived at the Leningradskaya Hotel at almost six thirty.

"You like this one, don't you, Natasha?" asked Aki

"Why? What makes you say that?"

"Oh I don't know… the way you couldn't take your eyes off him all evening, the way you only really wanted to talk to him, the way you forgot about the bridges, the way you told him my name was Aki… Why did you go and do that?"

"I don't know… I'd already made up my mind to tell him that I was Japanese, and I didn't want to be over here in the Soviet Union all on my own, so I chose you to be Japanese as well, and Aki was the first name I thought of. Sorry".

"I don't actually mind, I quite like the name, it's just that I've got to remember to react to it now… but you do like him, don't you? You went all mushy-brained and dewy-eyed".

"No I did not!"

"Yes, you did. It stood out a mile because I've never seen you like that before. Go on, admit it, you do like him, don't you?"

"Yes, all right, I do like him a bit, but I didn't go 'all mushy-brained and dewy-eyed'! I just went a little bit mushy-brained and dewy-eyed!" and they both laughed out loud.

"Good for you, Natasha".

"Was it that obvious?"

"It was to me, because it was so unusual for you, but I doubt whether Will noticed – he was in the same condition".

"Was he? Really? Oh, that's nice to know. Did you like Tom?"

"Yeah, he was all right. Nice enough to talk to and maybe practice position thirty-four with!" she bent double laughing as she said it and slapped her knees.

"You are awful, Aki, but I like you", said Natasha laughing, "I'm going for a bath".

When Youriko and Aki walked down the steps into the Evropeyskoe Bar at four fifteen, the boys were already there. Tom stood up quickly, kissed Aki and shook hands with Youriko. Will took his cue from his friend and greeted them in a similar fashion but the other way around.

"My shout, same as last night?" said Tom going to the bar.

"You're early", said Youriko.

"How so?" replied Will.

"Well, we agreed on the same time as yesterday and you got here at four thirty yesterday", she answered laughing.

He looked at her and saw that Aki was trying not to laugh as well. He wondered whether it was the Japanese sense of humour, otherwise, he didn't get it.

"In that case, you're both fifteen minutes late!" he said.

"Yes, we are!" giggled Aki.

"What's going on?" asked Tom returning with the drinks. "Has someone told a joke?"

"No, mate, I was just about to tell them about this morning".

"Yes, go on then, Will. Listen to this, girls".

"Well, we got back to the hotel at about half past six and our party was standing by a coach outside, so we paid the taxi driver and went over. Our head teacher, Dr. Tikhonov, pointed at us and screamed, 'There they are! Where the bloody Hell have you been?'. Excuse my French, but apparently, we were only booked into the Leningradskaya for one night, and the coach was there to bring us here. We're staying upstairs now.

"Well, we didn't know anything about it because we missed dinner when the move was announced. They didn't think too much about that, but when we missed our breakfast, they checked our room and saw that the beds hadn't been slept in, and someone said they'd seen us leaving the hotel minutes after getting there yesterday.

"So, Tikhonov reported it to the hotel, they called the police and the police called someone else and they were about to start a citywide sweep for us when we arrived…"

"Boy, Oh boy! Were they mad…"

"They questioned us separately and I said we went to a bar, crossed the river got stuck over there and some guy let us sleep on his floor. You said the same, didn't you, Tom?"

"Yes, I couldn't find my way back to your house, if I wanted to, but I'd never drop you in it, you said you weren't allowed male visitors. Old Sherlock, here could probably walk straight to your house blindfold though".

"Thanks, but I don't understand one hundred percent", said Aki so Tom explained the references.

"Ah", she said to Aki in Kazakh, "that's why there's that tail outside. Did you notice him?"

"Sure, I've seen him around several times. You reckon he's following these two?"

"Sure to be, they're going to be wondering how they knew their way around a city they've never been to before. They probably don't know that Will was here ten years ago and has the memory of an elephant. They'll be thinking that they slept at a contact's house as well".

"Yes, I think you're right… I wonder if that's the only resemblance Will bears to an elephant…"

"Aki!" she said slapping her shoulder playfully.

"What is it? Did I hear my name?" asked Will.

"Oh, it is nothing. Aki's English is not so good sometimes, so I must explain, but she likes to make jokes too. You heard your name? That is very keen hearing. You don't speak Kazakh, eh? Which languages do you speak?"

"English, Welsh, French, German, Latin and now I'm learning Russian. No Kazakh, sorry".

"So, five and a half, eh?"

Yes, and you?

"Twenty-two", she replied quietly.

"And the rest! She speaks twenty-two languages and six dialects fluently, don't you, Youriko?"

"Yes, I have always had a knack for languages, as do you, Will. Six languages is unusual for an Englishman, is it not?"

"Yes, it is, for a Welshman too. Tom and I are both Welsh".

"Ah, Wales, yes, I remember… the down-trodden Welsh coalminers oppressed by their English capitalist taskmasters. I should have known, you said you spoke Welsh".

"Mushy-brained", said Aki in Kazakh quietly and Youriko hit her again.

"What is it? Do tell?" said Tom.

"It's just Aki and her little jokes… they wouldn't translate well. Shall we take you to some real Russian bars or would you like to eat?"

"Bar!" they both said together.

"OK, but you have to eat too. I know just the place", she said in English and then to Aki "Let's see if that tail belongs to them".

They walked the fifteen feet from the entrances to the hotel and the bar up onto the Nevsky Prospekt and turned left, it was a good twenty minutes down the road and on the other side, so Natasha and Aki had plenty of opportunity to determine whether they were being followed.

As Youriko ushered her friends into the pub, the 'Kuvshin Peva', or 'Jug of Beer', she suddenly turned and looked the KGB man in the eyes and nodded. They knew each other vaguely from previous encounters in bars and restaurants when he had been following others. He gave the smallest and briefest of smiles and leaned against a wall to read the newspaper he was carrying for the purpose.

"He's theirs all right", she said to Aki as they bought vouchers that could be exchanged for beer and vodka in the bar, from where the loud sound of voices singing Russian folk songs was emanating.

They drank beer, sang songs and ate smoked roach, rudd and eels until eleven fifteen when the girls had to start back to get over the bridge.

"That was brilliant, I love that bar… the singing! It's like being back in Valleys, aye. We've got to go back in there more often and it's much cheaper than the Evropeyskoye Bar. They loved us in there as well, didn't they, Aki?" Aki agreed and it was true, they had been the centre of attention.

"They don't get many foreigners in there, especially not ones who can speak Russian. You were a novelty, but they liked you as well", said Aki.

They kissed and hugged their companions at the turning for their bridge before letting them run off to get over it just in time. "They're a great pair", said Will as they watched the girls disappear into the distance still running. "Tom," he asked, "have you ever seen a KGB man?"

"I don't think so, why do you say that?"

"When we turn to go to the hotel, look at the man on the corner across the road on our side of the Prospekt. Don't make it obvious. Now, see him? Youriko say's she spotted him following us from the Evropeyskaya Hotel. He's KGB".

"Wow! Now that's something I don't mind if you do tell everybody. It's never half measures with you, is it, boyo? Sleep on the floor in a house full of women one night and get followed home by a KGB agent the next. What've you got planned for tomorrow?"

"Ah, thanks for reminding me. Youriko is coming to the room at four thirty, so perhaps you could meet Aki in the bar downstairs on your own, and we'll join you there later?"

"You dirty, lucky sod!"

Andropov's Cuckoo

15 MUSHY-BRAINED AND DEWY-EYED

After class the next day, Tom went to the Evropeyskoye to meet Aki, and Youriko went up to Will's room. The babushka who sat by the lift and the stairs to control entry and report suspicious comings and goings to the KGB, blocked her progress, then phoned Will's room to check that it was all right to admit her. He gave his permission and waited for her in the doorway. He thought she was the most beautiful woman he had ever seen as he watched her walking towards him and when she smiled at him as if she sensed his thoughts, a soppy grin spread across his face.

"You look gorgeous", he said, "come on in. Are you well?"

"Yes, thanks and you? What are you doing?"

"Sewing a new patch on my jeans. I brought it with me because I knew the knee wouldn't last much longer". He sat on the bed again and took up his sewing, it was the nearest seat to the large bay windows, the best source of light. "Take a seat".

She sat next to him on the bed and put part of his trousers across her lap. "Do you mind if I give you some advice?" she asked shyly.

"No, not at all, give me a kiss and tell me what it is". They pecked, like couples do in the morning.

"It's just that your stitching is too far apart. This will not last, it is not strong. Will you let me do it for you? I haven't sewn for years, not since I used to sew with my grandmothers as a child".

"Be my guest", he said and put an arm around her waist as she assessed the task. He watched as she matched the spacing of his stitching going around the circular patch of Hendrix playing guitar and then went around again putting another stitch between the first ones. It took her ten minutes despite the interference from Will's left hand on her back. When she was done, she tried to break the double thread but could not, she also tried biting through it, but in vain.

"Unbreakable nylon thread", he offered.

"Have you got any scissors?" she asked.

"What student takes scissors on holiday?" he replied and pulled a three-inch penknife from his pocket. He opened it, but was watching what he was doing not his companion. Her eyes opened wide and fear twisted across her no longer beautiful face. As he went to hand her the knife she dropped to her knees on the floor crying, moaning some words he didn't understand.

"What is it, Youriko? What is it, girl?" He hugged her to his knees and kissed the top of her head many, many times until she stopped crying and shaking. He slipped to the floor covering her legs with his, enveloping her body in his large frame. "What is it, Youriko, my dear? Please tell me".

She didn't come out of his protective cocoon, but held him tight and between genuine sobs, told him the story of her life in a hushed voice directly into his ear. She told him the truth about her life in Alma Ata and her mother; about school, university and Yui; she related her experiences in the Japanese foreign office and her move to Bonn and she told him about the loneliness of her job and her attempted escape to California. She wasn't doing this for sympathy, she was unburdening a story that she had never told anyone ever before, and because he was making all the right noises in all the right places, yet hadn't interrupted nor released her, she dared to continue.

"From all the stories I've heard about the Lubyanka, I was treated well there. I kept expecting more to happen to me, but I was basically just left to slither about in spilt food, dampness and my own mess. It was completely degrading. Then they allowed me to hope that I would soon be freed, but it was only another trick to break me down. I was sentenced to five years at a corrective labour camp north of Moscow. The guards could do anything they liked to you for any reason, in fact they didn't even need a reason.

"If you complained or they even thought you might, two guards would hold you and another would shoot you in the back, dead, eh, wounded was no good. Then they could claim a reward for stopping a runaway. They didn't need an excuse. We used to joke that if baby needed new shoes, they would shoot someone to pay for them.

"Others were just naturally sadistic. Look", she said holding her beautifully manicured nails towards him and then turning her hands around. "See those red lines, er, scars behind my nails? That's where a man pushed his penknife down and flipped my nails out. You surely want to know what I had done to deserve this treatment, eh? Well, I cannot tell you, because I do not know. Perhaps, his wife had shouted at him that morning. When things like this happened for no reason, we just used to say that it was 'his turn'. Well, I got my turn sometimes too and so did everybody else. Pull my hair back... no, like this, see that line? I was beaten by guards with sticks so hard that my hair won't grow there any longer... Why? It was just my turn.

"Seeing you with a knife like that brought it all back, it does sometimes, and usually when I'm least expecting it". She started to pull her top off. "Please make love to me now! I need you, I need to hold and feel someone who cares. You do care, don't you, Will?"

"Yes", he said. He had hoped they would end up in bed, but he had never imagined that it would come about like this. To say that he was distracted by her story was no exaggeration, but her passion soon rekindled his ardour, until they lay on the bed exhausted.

Youriko fell asleep holding him tight with her arms and her legs, but sleep would not come to Will as he played and replayed his lover's story over and over again. He had read books and heard stories on TV, but it was unbelievable that he was holding someone it had actually happened to. This was no story, this was the Truth.

As he lay there thinking, there came a sudden knock on the door. Tom's face appeared in the crack. "Are you decent?"

"No, come back in thirty minutes". He heard a female giggling outside, probably Aki, he thought. When the door had closed, he woke Youriko; they made love again quickly, showered, tidied Will's bed and left the room for Tom and Aki.

From that moment, they were inseparable. They walked hand in hand, kissed in public and generally behaved as young courting couples do. Love-making at four thirty became a fixture and sometimes, they hired another room for the weekend so the could just be together. They were completely besotted with one another, and she told him every little detail about herself, even her real age, but no matter what her feelings were, she never broke her promise to her controller about revealing the true nature of her job. She was never going back to a camp again for anyone.

After a few days, the tail was called off, partly because the two students no longer displayed suspicious behaviour and partly because Youriko had vouched for them. They were happy because it gave them an extra man to put on someone else. However, Will completely surprised her one morning when he asked for help with an errand he had promised to perform while in the UK.

"I met a dissident friend of one of my lecturers a few months back," he said, "a Viktor Fainberg. Have you heard of him? He was one of the seven dissidents, along with Natalya Gorbanevskaya, who protested on the Red Square against the invasion of Czechoslovakia in 1968. Yuri Andropov had them all beaten up, arrested and either thrown into jail or into corrective labour camps. Sorry, to bring that up. Have you heard of him now, or Natalya, sorry, I can't remember the other's names... Have you heard of Andropov?"

"No, I've never heard of any of them", she lied for the benefit of the microphone hidden in the radio or pendant light. She put a finger to his lips and mouthed the word 'microphone'. He caught on, felt stupid and kissed her. "Ah, well, never mind all that rubbish", he said in a normal voice, let's go for a walk.

"Good idea". she agreed. When they were on the Nevsky Prospekt, Will continued his story.

"Anyway, Viktor wants me to get a letter to his son, who's also called Yuri. I have a phone number, a letter of introduction and a personal, sealed letter for him. How would I best go about it?"

"Are you mad? The best thing you can do is burn it and forget about it!"

"I can't do that, I gave my word. I realise why you're frightened, so I'll do it on my own, I expected to have to anyway".

"So, how are you going to do that?"

"I'll phone him and arrange a meeting?"

"All the hotel phones will be bugged, you know that, surely?"

"Yes, I forgot. I'll use a street phone then".

"Yes, but not one outside a hotel, because they'll be bugged as well. Have you noticed whether you're still being followed?"

"I don't think I am..."

"If you are, you'll lead them straight to Fainberg's son, if he is in hiding. He might not be".

"This is why I asked for your advice, you know more about these things than I do".

"Yes, but when you go home, they might put me back in prison". He had been banning thoughts of going home from his mind.

"I don't want to put you under any risk whatsoever, Youriko, that is written in stone!" he assured her.

"No, I'm sure you don't, my love, but just by thinking about this and holding those letters, that is what you are doing". She thought about it for a few moments, "No, I am most sorry, my dear, but I cannot be a part of this. I will go home now, please make your arrangements and make the delivery in public places. Do not, under any circumstances, be persuaded to meet them in some safe house or park. I will look for you tomorrow night in the Jug at nine. These matters are best transacted swiftly. I'll see you tomorrow, if all goes well, and make sure that Tom knows the arrangements, you don't want to be on your own in this".

Her hope was that Will would tell Tom his plans and she would ask Aki to wheedle them out of him, so that she could follow in the background and keep an eye on him, because he was playing a dangerous game but didn't realise it. He was his own worst enemy, an ignorant man who didn't realise that he was ignorant.

He phoned the number from a call box up the road and spoke to a very nervous young man in Russian. Viktor had said that his son had spent years in state psychiatric institutions, not because of his mental health but because his father was one of 'The Seven'. The KGB was trying to coax Viktor to go back to help his son so they could arrest him.

Will arranged to meet him at four thirty outside the Evropeyskoye Bar and told Tom, who told Aki et cetera. Youriko stood across the Prospekt in disguise with a camera so she could witness what happened. She saw a man of about twenty-two shuffle past Will in a battered raincoat and she saw Will look him in the eyes, but then the man moved hurriedly on. Will looked as if he were about to follow him, when another young man in a very smart raincoat carrying an umbrella approached him. Will told her later what had happened.

"William Davies? I am Viktor's son, I believe you have a letter for me. How is my dear papa?"

Will played for time, "Can we talk somewhere?" he had asked.

"Sure, the European Bar, it is my favourite". So they had gone there.

The man had ordered the drinks and paid for them in American dollars, but alarms were going off in Will's head one after the other. This man was clean-cut, strong upright and muscular, spoke English perfectly, had foreign currency and said he drank there frequently, but Russians weren't allowed to have foreign currency or to be in valuta bars, plus the man he had spoken to before stuttered from nervousness and spoke English haltingly. Will had taken three drinks off him, said there was no letter only a verbal message and told him how well Viktor was doing. When the man left, Will had been right behind him, and saw him jump into a chauffeured limousine and leave at speed up the Prospekt.

Youriko had been about to cross the road to ask what had happened, when the first man had appeared again and stopped by Will staring at him, with the sad sunken eyes of the persecuted.

"You know my father?" he had asked.

"Viktor? Yes, he is well and thinks of you every day". Tears had welled up in the young man's eyes, whereas the other man had reacted as if he heard from his father every day. She saw him reach into his inside pocket and hand over a letter or two, then the other man had shuffled off at treble time.

Both Will and Youriko were certain that the right man had got the message. She crossed the road and followed her hero into the Evropeyskoye Bar, the European Bar as the imposter Yuri had called it in translation.

"What a fantastic surprise", he said as she entered the empty bar. "I've just had the weirdest experience of my life".

"I saw some of it, tell me the rest". En route to the ladies toilet when Will had finished his story, she lent over the bar, "Was the guy earlier KGB?"

"Yes, comrade, one of us, but a real high-flyer".

"Thanks, I thought so".

Tom and Aki joined them fresh from the hotel room at five fifteen and while the girls were discussing recent events, and Youriko was playing them down, Tom told Will about an idea he had had.

"You know how handy it is to have a language that no-one around you can speak?"

"Yes, but we're stuffed here, aren't we? The girls speak all of ours except Welsh and you can't speak that very well".

"No, but there is another way. When I was a kid in Pyle, we used to use 'eggy slang', did you?"

"No, I've never heard of 'eggy slang', what is it?"

"It's dead simple, but it should throw everyone here. You just add 'egg' before every vowel. Like, er, 'Eggi weggant teggo geggo teggo thegge teggoileggett'. Get it? 'I want to go to the toilet'. Have a practice, I won't be long".

After he returned, he and Will practised, and it seemed to work and when Youriko asked them what language they were speaking, Tom said Welsh.

Will had one more surprise for Youriko, which he revealed as they were walking to the bridge that night.

"I was given a dozen Bibles to hand out by one of my lecturers", he said one night, "who would want them the most, do you think?"

"Oh, my God! You're a real liability, aren't you? Still, it's not as bad as the last surprise. How many more shocks have you got in stone for me?"

"This is it, love, one dozen Bibles".

Youriko found out when a wedding was going to be held in one of the smaller churches just out of the city centre and they 'just happened to be passing' while it was taking place. They waited for the couple to come out with the priest and then Will ran over the road to present him with a plastic Tesco's carrier bag of Bibles. He didn't wait for the astonished priest to open the bag, but Youriko said that the expression on his face was priceless as he looked up to Heaven and gave thanks.

Their love, or infatuation, and mutual respect deepened in no time. They spent hundreds of hours plotting how they could get her out to Britain, but the only way that seemed feasible was marriage. They were both prepared, no enthusiastic, to take that approach, but there was no time to find out how to go about it and arrange it, if it were indeed possible. Youriko was far more realistic than Will, so had seen the day of their separation coming from the moment that she had thrown her hat in with him, but it all seemed to be something of a surprise to Will.

He was such an innocent in many ways, but she was glad that she had met him, because he had renewed her faith that human beings could be nice and even altruistic. However, most of all he had awakened a fire in her that she had seen in other men and women over the years, but which she herself had never found anyone who could ignite. She didn't believe in God, but she prayed to Him anyway just in case, that she would see this man again after he had to go back.

She knew that he felt the same because the emotion from him was stronger than she had ever realised was possible.

One afternoon, a fortnight before he had to return, it was her turn to surprise him again. She had her period, the first one since meeting him. They were still irregular, but they were becoming more normal as her lifestyle normalised too. She didn't know how he felt about periods, so she took an unusual action. When she knocked on his hotel room door, she had a friend with her who sat on a chair by the doorway, but said nothing. Youriko didn't introduce her or mention her, but kissed Will and started their prequel to making love as usual.

Will thought it was very odd, but didn't like to say anything, and Youriko kept his back to the girl as she undressed him, pushed him onto the bed and took her own clothes off, all but her panties. She held his head to face her and coaxed him to an erection with the other. Then she held his penis upright, pulled the foreskin back and the other girl let it slide into her naked body.

"Don't look at her, darling, pretend it's me, squeeze my breasts and kiss me. Tell me you love me! That is me up there… Oh, I love you, I love you so much, my darling".

When he had finished, the girl got off and dressed. Youriko went over to her and let her out.

Will had no idea why that had just happened, but guessed that Youriko's friend wanted a baby and she was helping her.

So had he.

"What was that all about, love. A bit weird, wasn't it?"

"I have my period", she said as if that explained everything.

"Yes, and?"

"Well, I didn't know how you felt about making love when a woman has a period, and I know you like to make love, so… It's an old, ancient Kazakh custom… if you love your man, you will do anything for him. Did I not please you, Will?"

"It's not that…, you certainly surprised me though, so did she when she slid down over me…"

"That was not another woman, that was me", she said huffily as she started to get dressed.

"I'm sorry, Youriko, it's just something I'm not used to. It was a lovely gesture on your part. Thanks for thinking of me", he kissed her on the forehead and squeezed one of her breasts.

"I choose a girl who was pretty, but not as pretty as me, and I could have got one a little younger", she giggled, but it was a gesture, I didn't want you to enjoy yourself too much, and I didn't want to make myself jealous. I said to her, 'My man has a big thing, but if I see you enjoying yourself or if you make one sound to make him think you are, I will not pay you!

"Now, let me wash you in the shower and we can go for a drink with Tom and Aki".

While the boys were talking to each other and so were the girls, Will suddenly put his finger on Tom's knee to stop him talking. He looked at his friend and tuned an ear to the girls' conversation. 'Listen', he mouthed.

"Well, blow me down!" exclaimed Tom, "Would you believe it? They're using 'eggy slang' in Russian".

"What's the matter?" asked Youriko in eggy Russian "Shteggo slegguchegileggos?"

"Nothing", replied Will, "when did you crack our code?"

"The same night when we were walking home over the bridge. We've been using it in Russian now and again for weeks wondering when you would notice". First, the girls started laughing and then the boys had to join in.

"You didn't really believe that a simple trick like that would fool a woman who has learned on average more than one language a year since the day that she was born, did you, boys?" laughed Aki. "Oh, dear me, you have no idea how bright this woman is, you really don't, do you? She's absolutely brilliant!"

Youriko was reddening under her friend's praise and the obvious adoration from Will, but she was proud of it too.

"It was nothing, really", she sad shyly, "it just came to me, that's all".

The day before he had to leave, they made love all morning and all afternoon in another hotel, then they went shopping for gifts for his friends and family and for each other.

She was allowed to go to the airport on the coach to see him off, because everyone knew how close they had become. Youriko stayed looking out of the window for several hours after the plane had left. She had felt loneliness many times in her life and each time it had plumbed new depths, but this was too deep. It hurt more than she could imagine.

Will had promised to find out about getting her out of the Soviet Union by marriage and he had promised to return the following year, although it would be to Kalinin, not Leningrad and they had promised to write, but she knew how hit and miss that could be. She wished Will another silent farewell, blew him a kiss and returned to the real world that she had inhabited before she had met him. His lasting impact would be that he had taught her that even she was capable of loving and being loved and for that she knew she would be eternally grateful.

She looked for a taxi home with a heavy heart, she wanted to get drunk with her friends but she had lost track of them in the last week. She was also well behind with her paperwork, so she told the taxi driver to take her home. However, as they were about to turn right over the bridge she changed her mind and descended from the cab down into the Evropeyskoye for a few night caps and a cry to herself before walking across the bridge home again.

She knew that her life would never be the same again and she found that frightening without Will at her side.

Will, for his part, sat on the plane home, also feeling more lonely than he had ever felt before. He had had many girlfriends, but none that had made him feel the way that Youriko had. He had no idea how to achieve his goal, but he was determined to get her out of the Soviet Union and into his life in the UK or wherever he might end up.

While his friends were talking about what a great holiday and how many girls they had had, he felt strangely superior to them that they had had quantity, which he had normally gone for as well, whereas he had met a woman the like of which there were few in the world.

16 SOCHI, KRASNODARSKAYA KRAI

The following four months in Leningrad passed painfully for Youriko. Everywhere she went reminded her of Will and she couldn't bear even the thought of another man touching her. She wrote him a letter and sent it to the address he had given her, and while she waited anxiously for a reply, she sent him a postcard every few days, but she never received a reply to any of her missives. She couldn't understand it.

She hadn't put a return address on her letter, because she had given him the address of the house he had slept at that first night and she didn't want any intercepted mail to be traceable back to her. She didn't put her address on the postcards either, but then who did?

'Surely it hadn't just been a holiday romance for him?' she wondered over and over again. 'Surely, her instincts couldn't have been that wrong?'

She decided that her letters were not getting through. 'The KGB was blocking them', she reasoned, 'but why would they block a few love letters from him or from her?' It. was, after all, part of her remit to get in deep with her 'clients', which, as far as her superiors knew, was all Will was. They didn't know that she had fallen for this one. She had filed a report on him in the normal way, but had not provided as much detail as she normally would have. Anyway, she thought, if she got out and married him, they could hardly blackmail him with information that he had been sleeping with his girlfriend.

Eventually, after months of waiting, she concluded that it just wasn't going to be easy and that she would have to wait until the following year when Will and the rest of his class were returning to the Soviet Union. He had said that they had been told that they would be studying in Kalinin from early June 1979 until the end of August.

She plodded on doing her job, but without the enthusiasm she had had before meeting Will. Christmas, although not a Soviet celebration was celebrated by the tourists and the government had tried to fold it into the New Year, so it was a highlight on the calendar and an opportunity to forget one's woes and have a good time. Youriko tried hard and even succeeded a couple of times, but in the first week of January, when the quiet season started, she and her team were recalled to Moscow for a break, a debriefing and reassignment.

At the first meeting with the top controller, the one who was in charge of the two who controlled the teams, she met a new team leader, whose name was Katya, and she saw her old friend Irina.

"How are you, Irina?"

"Fantastic! We've just had a marvellous year in Krasnodar. You wait till you get down there, you'll love it. Look at this suntan, it's not fake, you know… Where were you, Leningrad, wasn't it? Any good?"

"The suntan suits you. Yes, we were in Leningrad… it's very nice, very cultural. It's the most beautiful city I've ever seen in Russia. I wonder where they'll be sending us next".

"I think we're going to find out this evening. Here he comes now, we'd better be quiet".

He gave a long speech about how successful the venture had been and how well everyone had done and then came the section that the team leaders were waiting for.

"Before we get to the part you are naturally most concerned to hear, your reassignments, I have a surprise for you. We have recruited sixty-six more operatives, one of whom is here now. Comrade Katya, that is Comrade Youriko and that is Comrade Irina. You three will lead the new enlarged teams. You will each have five teams of five girls working for you. You should choose one girl in every group to report back to you at least once a week, twice is better, and you will collate all this data and pass it on to your controller once a week unless asked for a special report.

"An innovation that we are working on is a gay team of men, perhaps a lesbian team will follow or perhaps that won't be necessary if you have the right mix of female team members. However, we will be relying on your feedback on this matter, so noses to the grindstone but ears to the ground, eh, eh?"

"It is understood that you three will have an increased amount of administration, so you will not be expected to be on, shall we say, active service any longer, unless you find that you have the time, of course.

"And now, what you have all been waiting for: Katya, you and your team will be going to Leningrad, please see Youriko for any tips she can give you; Youriko, you will be in Krasnodarskaya Krai, you can talk to Irina, and Irina, you will be in Kalinin. No-one has spent a full term there yet, but Youriko and Katya did a few weeks training there, so they may be able to help you, but basically, you will have to play it by ear, I'm afraid.

"Any questions?"

"Yes, comrade!" said Youriko, "May we swap assignments? I know that Comrade Irina had great success in Krasnodarskaya Krai, why not allow her to stay there and I will go to Kalinin in her place?"

"No, I am afraid that that is out of the question. Our extensive research in other fields indicates that after a year in one place, the faces of the operatives become too well known by those who go there regularly, which results in lower productivity. Here are your envelopes with instructions, you have three days to prepare, then you leave for your destinations en masse on Saturday morning.

"I have one more surprise for you. I am very pleased to announce that in light of your past success and in recognition of your elevated rôles as leaders of much-enlarged teams, you are to be given a rank in the KGB. You are now officially sergeants in the KGB. Congratulations!

"We are looking into making each of your five team leaders corporals and each of their team members privates, but that will depend a lot on your recommendations and observations, the quality, that is the reliability and accuracy, of which will determine your own prospects of future promotion, as will, of course, the quality of the information your whole team has gathered.

"This is a big honour, and I will admit, one that took me totally by surprise, but I am assured that the idea came right from the very top, Comrade Andropov, who is now your ultimate Commander-in-Chief. Show your gratitude by excelling in your work and you will do well, because you are being watched from the very Kremlin itself. You will not be issued with uniforms, but you will be given KGB warrant cards, which will get you or your team members out of difficulty if they are arrested for being in valuta bars or such like". He motioned to his aide, who handed out the three cards in leather wallets. "Full instructions are in your envelopes. Once again, comrades, congratulations!"

"Now, I must leave, so, good evening, and good luck", and with that he briskly left the room with his aide.

The three women were all inspecting the red leather wallets they had just been handed. They had the star, hammer and sickle emblem and KGB CCCP embossed in gold on the front and contained two identity cards issued by the Moscow Division, Andropov's own district. Katya and Irina were stunned, but obviously ever so proud. Youriko didn't know their backgrounds, but they were unlikely to have been like hers, so it was right that they should feel proud of such a promotion, but she just felt bewildered and heart-broken.

All her plans were dashed, although she was glad that she had a legitimate excuse for remaining true to her Will.

Over the next few days, she spent the daytime training her new members and the evenings getting to know them. She put each of the 'original girls' in charge of four new ones to make up the required teams. Everyone was excited to be going to the most luxurious holiday destination in the Soviet Union. Everyone but Youriko, who would rather have given anything to be staying eighteen hundred kilometres north of the Black Sea holiday resorts.

Still, the day came and all her attempts at behind the scenes coaxing didn't change anything, so the twenty-six of them boarded their flight and headed down south. It was like a teacher taking a class of exuberant teenagers on an outing. Most of the girls had never been anywhere before; they seemed young and fresh-faced. She guessed that they had probably been recruited from farming communities and villages, they made the thirty-year-old Youriko feel like a frumpy Old Maid, and the plain fact of the matter was that she was at least ten years older than most of them, their ages ranging from eighteen to twenty-two.

However, Youriko liked the way that her job had developed. She hadn't minded cavorting with men, but she had always felt awkward with sleeping with them in order to obtain information. It had always been the last resort for her and only then if she was certain that that the man had something worthwhile to offer and there was no other means of getting it. She had never gone to bed with men easily, not even before the camp, but that experience had made it much, much more difficult.

She didn't know why she had always 'held back', she guessed she had been shy, and then just got used to being alone. Until she met Will. He had changed all that in a matter of hours and their six weeks together had been the happiest of her life. She had thought that she had made him happy too, but after five months without any contact, she was beginning to have her doubts.

Youriko's girls were billeted in 'family rooms' in five holiday resorts in and around Sochi in Krasnodarskaya Krai on the Black Sea, while she had her own small single chalet with some basic office equipment. They were all within ten kilometres either side of her, so she could easily travel to see how they were getting along on a regular basis. They were primarily tasked with finding out how heavily the locals were involved in smuggling, and who was behind it, until the holiday season got underway in May, when they would switch their attention to specific Russian targets chosen by the controller, and then the foreigners would start to arrive in greater numbers in June and July.

Her new, more administrative rôle, kept her busy, perhaps a lot busier than was necessary, but she didn't want any free time on her hands. As June approached, she joked with herself that she was beginning to understand what deer must feel like as the rutting season draws near.

From June the first, she couldn't bear the thought that Will was in the country, but not with her.

She spent an hour one evening, copying out the phone numbers of all the bars and hotels in Kalinin, then she walked around town phoning them from call boxes she thought were 'clean'. She had no joy, nobody had heard of a William Davies, and the majority of students were American and Canadian. So, she waited a week and tried again, but the result was the same. She phoned Irina several times and asked her to look out for Will, but none of her crew had met him. On one occasion, she mentioned that the Americans and Canadians were going home the following week, so she would try again then.

On a whim, she rang the Evropeyskoye Bar and spoke to the barman. It was the same one and he remembered her and Will.

"Yes, I know the man, I should do, he's been in here every evening for a fortnight asking after you. When I say I haven't seen you, his chin hits his chest, he gets legless and goes. I told him I haven't seen you for what? Six months, is it?"

"Yes, just about. Where is he staying?"

"They left for Moscow this morning..."

"Moscow or Kalinin?"

"I don't know, comrade, all the same, isn't it? He'd have to go to Moscow and then come back out to Kalinin, wouldn't he?"

"Yes, that's true, but will he be staying in Moscow or Kalinin... eventually?"

"I don't know, sorry, maybe he did mention Kalinin... yes, come to think of it, I think he did".

"Thanks, if he phones or comes back tell him I'm looking for him and give him this number... Thanks a lot, I owe you a drink, comrade, bye".

She cursed herself for not having thought of just trying the Evropeyskoye Bar on speculation, he had been there two weeks and looking for her while she had been searching for him seven hundred kilometres away. She looked at her watch, it was nine ten, he was probably there by now, but where?

She phoned the hotels only and was told that there were no British there. It was incredibly frustrating. She wanted to get on a plane and walk from hotel to hotel and bar to bar until she found him. His stay in Russia was ticking away quickly and six weeks hadn't been nearly long enough the last time.

On the Monday, her daily round of phone calls to hotels in Kalinin produced affirmation that a party of British students had arrived that morning, but she could not confirm that a William Davies was among them. However, it was enough for her. She had been working out what she would do when she located him, so she swang that plan into action.

She met with her controller every Saturday afternoon to submit the weekly report and discuss any issues. It normally took an hour or two. She had arranged with Aki, that from there she would fly to Moscow and go to Kalinin to see Will, but would be back by Friday to write up the report. Aki was to keep the operation ticking over and tell people that Youriko had phoned to say that she was sick. They joked that if asked to be specific, Aki could say anything but lovesick. Aki had agreed to help willingly, but Youriko made her promise not to put her neck on the line.

"If you are missed, Youriko, you know that the consequences could be severe?"

"Yes, Aki, but I have to go. He is the only man I have ever loved and he loves me back… I can't not see him while he's here… You understand that, don't you?"

"Yes, I do… I hope that one day I will love someone that much again and that he will love me back. Good luck to you, my friend, give me a hug… Maybe some of your good luck will rub off on me. Don't worry about here, I'll make sure you are not missed".

She wrote herself a travel permit from the booklet she used to allow the girls to travel with their marks, signed some for Aki to dispense and flew to Moscow, from where she took a bus to Kalinin. When she arrived late at night, she booked into a small guest house, phoned Aki and went to bed certain that she was close to her Will again at last.

After breakfast, she started out with a spring in her step, hope in her heart and a list of hotels in her bag, but by lunchtime, the prospect of finding him looked as dim as ever. The only hotel that had a contingent of British students staying did not have a William Davies. She showed the receptionist a photo of them together to prove that she had a right to be enquiring after him, but the receptionist started to get angry and said the answer was still negative.

She did a tour of the bars for the rest of the day, but despite finding British students, nobody knew the man in the photo or had heard of a William Davies. It was devastating news and all she could do was go back to Sochi a few days early.

Still, as time was running out, she kept phoning around but kept hearing the same story. It was as if he and his fellow students had been spirited away.

In the last week of August when she had all but given up hope, she received a phone call in her room after work.

"Is that you, Youriko?"

"Will, my darling, where are you? Wherever have you been? I've been searching for you for weeks".

"I'm in the Evropeyskoye, the barman just gave me your phone number. So much precious time has been lost. We're going back home the day after tomorrow".

"I'll fly up tomorrow, we will have a night together. Where are you staying?"

"The Evropeyskaya again, we arrived this morning from Strelna, a resort, just around the coast outside Leningrad."

"Yes, I know it, but what about Kalinin?"

"We were there, two weeks in Leningrad, two weeks in Kalinin, a week in Moscow, a week in the resort, three days here and then home".

Youriko made the same arrangements with Aki and took the next possible flight, the seven am to Leningrad, Will met her at the airport and it was obvious that nothing had changed between then. Will booked another room in the Evropeyskaya and they didn't leave it until she took him to the airport the following afternoon. It was such a pleasure to be in each other's arms once more, but the time they had was so short.

"Why didn't you answer any of my letters or postcards, darling", she asked after they had made love.

"I am ashamed to tell you that, my ex-girlfriend came around to pick up some of her things and we shared a bottle of wine. I told her about you and showed her your photos and stuff, remember, it was all in one bag? Anyway, she stayed the night, she said she was too drunk to go home, and when I woke up in the morning she set fire to all your details. She had them in the sink soaked in turpentine ready to set light to. The piece of paper you gave me with your address on it was in there too".

"If you're not staying with me, you're not having her instead', she said. "I'm sorry, my love, I was so stupid... I should have seen that it would make her jealous".

"There, don't worry about it now, at least we've found each other again, even if only for a brief while".

When he asked what she was doing and where, she said that she was running a team of tour guides on the Black Sea holiday resort of Sochi. She still did not dare to break her promise, never to divulge the true nature of her work.

Youriko could not, would not give this man up, but what could she do? She was a marked woman, even though they had given her a rank in the KGB. By the time she landed at Sochi airport the vaguest threads of a plan were dangling before her consciousness, but they were still way out of reach.

17 THE FULL BOTTLE

She instinctively knew that Will had told her the truth about why he hadn't replied to her correspondence. It was all or nothing now, because if she was caught doing anything illegal that could be construed to be anti-Soviet or 'against the state', she could expect to be worked to death or even shot, although the alternative of living without the only person who had ever made her feel so alive, was no less frightening.

Youriko spent a lot of her free time reading the reports that she and the girls had submitted on smuggling and corrupt local officials and she told the team-leaders to tell their girls not to stop listening out for any further information on the subjects that might come their way. Naturally, she could not redirect the focus of their operation all together, but there would be no harm in remaining alert to local crime and corrupt officials.

She pored over reports of alleged people-trafficking from the southern Caucasus into Turkey, Greece and Arab countries. Many of these people, it was said, were to be used in the sex industry and forced-labour camps. She definitely didn't want to get caught up with criminal gangs like that, but there were other types of smuggling going on as well such as marijuana, gold, silver, guns and even caviar.

One of the problems she could foresee besides being caught trying to escape, being handed over to the authorities for a reward or being sold into slavery, was the fact that the rouble was not convertible, so if she decided to try to get out, she would be penniless again. She needed more liquid funds and an idea came to her.

Often, foreign tourists would give small items of gold or jewellery as a memento to a girl he had stayed with for a week or two and formed a bond with. She let it be known that she was in the market for all these precious items. It was a good deal for the girls who usually sold them anyway, but then had to find a private buyer or sell them through an agency that was a front for the government, meaning that the bureaucracy knew even more about them.

She soon had a dozen or so gold and silver bracelets, necklaces and rings and two foreign watches in place of the money that Andropov had given her back from the old days before the camp. She hoped that the reduction in her bank balance would go unnoticed for a while, since she had paid for the items over several weeks. She also needed a detailed map of Georgia and the western region of it known as Abkhazia.

She ruled out trying to cross the Black Sea, as she was well aware of the many patrol boats and the ruthlessness with which they treated people trying to leave the Soviet Union illegally. The story was that some boats were fired upon and sunk, and the crews left to drown. Still, she hoped to be able to use one of the smugglers to get her out somehow.

As she was copying the names of suspect smugglers onto a clean sheet of paper for later use, another thought crossed her mind. She had already reported these people, so some may be behind bars, others may be under surveillance and yet others may even be dead! Except as a group of names not to go to, the list was useless, she had reduced her own chances of escape with the efficiency of her team.

It was a bitter realisation and a massive stumbling block.

The managers and the senior staff at the hotels where her teams were based knew who Youriko and her friends were, and so treated her as a colleague in the vast network of the surveillance industry that operated wherever tourists gathered, both foreign and Soviet. She learned that they were in the high season for runaways, because not many people fancied their chances of survival in the mountains of the Caucasus or Georgia during the bitter winter months, which would soon be upon them.

Everybody had their favourite horror stories concerning a runaway who had been tortured or shot, or thrown himself off a cliff rather than face the consequences of getting caught trying to flee to Turkey, which was most people's target country. The dead bodies of presumed attempted escapees were often washed up on beaches, some had been shot, some had drowned and others had died of exhaustion.

Some even said that there were miniature submarines in the sea, the sole purpose of which was to seek and destroy Russian boats trying to cross over, while others claimed that there were mine fields with secret passageways known only to fishermen and the patrol boats of the navy and the coast guards. Runaway boats, some laughed, were used by the navy and coastal batteries for live target practise. They didn't stand a chance, no-one made it across the water. If a boat didn't have a registered call sign or markings it was presumed guilty and sunk.

Youriko wasn't sure she believed all these stories, but there was obviously a lot of surveillance, she had seen the fast boats and the light aircraft on patrol from the picture windows of all the resorts she visited. No, it would have to be by land, she was quite sure of that.

Sitting in the bar at her resort one Thursday afternoon waiting for Aki and the four other team leaders to arrive for their weekly get together, she had an idea. She still didn't know whether her parents were alive. She hadn't cared one way or the another about her mother for the last four years, but she still had fond memories of her father teaching her to ride a horse and play chess as a child. She asked for the hotel telephone to be brought to her.

"Can I use this for long distance to Alma Ata? I've just realised I haven't spoken to my parents for ages and it looks as if I've got a few minutes to spare", she asked the waitress.

"Yes, Comrade Youriko, all the public telephones for use by the clientele can... not abroad though", she said with a look on her face that said 'you should know that already'. She dialled the number that they had had since their phone had been installed and to her surprise and joy, it rang.

"Good afternoon", said a shaky male voice.

"Comrade Pyotr Myrskii?" she enquired. "Dad?"

"Tasha? It can't be..." she heard him fighting back a wave of sobs.

"Yes, it's me, Tasha, Dad... Sorry I haven't called for so long... How are you?" Tears were in her eyes too now. The waitress who had been standing, watching smiled and walked away slightly embarrassed at her intrusion.

"Oh, up and down, you know. I've finished work now and life's a bit quiet sometimes, especially since your mother passed away".

"Mum has died? Oh, I didn't know. When?"

"About two years ago now... she got sick about four years ago, but the doctors couldn't find anything wrong with her, so couldn't cure it. She couldn't work, lost her job and just got sicker and sicker, until one day she gave up. I think she just gave up anyway. She just lost the will to live… drank too much, smoked too much… you know how it goes. I don't know what made her go that way. We'd drifted apart a lot by then and didn't confide in each other any more. I still miss her though… We were together for forty years… it's a long time, you know?"

"Yes, Dad, it is a long time. I'm really sorry to hear she passed away. How are you coping?"

"All right, I guess. I don't want much. I can make my own breakfast… a woman down the corridor brings me dinner and does my laundry, you know? And I read or watch television until it's time to go to sleep. I don't get out much now… What are you doing these days?"

"I'm working in Sochi, Dad, as a group leader for a bunch of tour guides… I'm waiting for a meeting with them at this very moment, and I thought, I'll ring my dear old Dad. I was remembering you teaching me to ride and play chess… so, I thought I'd call you". She was crying again and the girls behind the bar were watching. "Look, Dad, I've got to go now, the others are arriving. I'll phone you very soon, all right? Look after yourself! Lots of love… Yes, you too. Bye…" she whispered and hung up.

"Finished?" asked the waitress wanting to return the phone to its usual resting place.

"Yes, thanks".

"Bad news?" she asked with a concerned look on her face.

"My mother died recently and my father is upset… he's all alone now… I'm the only child and I'm four and a half thousand kilometres away… I'm not much use to him here".

"Ah, that's sad", she replied not being able to help, so picking up the phone and walking off.

When the other five girls walked in a few minutes later, they all kissed and hugged, laughed and told stories, while Youriko ordered a jug of Sangria and six glasses to be placed on a table in the corner over by the huge picture window that looked out over the Black Sea from high above the beach. Anybody seeing them together would have thought they were an all-female sales team comparing notes after a week's work, and they wouldn't have been that far off the mark.

"This is definitely the best view of any of the resorts", cooed one of the girls. "You're so lucky, Youriko! Eh! Your mascara's been running! What's the matter, you been crying? You've been crying, your eyes are all puffy. Who's done this to you?"

"Leave her alone, Mitzi", said Aki. "What's the matter, Youriko?" she asked her friend quietly. Nobody else uttered a word, which was very unusual.

"Oh", she said with a heavy sigh, "I just heard from my Dad that my mother died. She's been sick quite a while, but Dad is taking it badly. I feel so sorry for him stuck in his flat all alone… He says he can't get out much and just watches TV all day until it's time to go to bed again. Not much of a life for a war hero who's worked all his life, is it?"

"Of course you feel sorry for him, he's your Dad, the poor old bloke… it's a crying shame", said Mitzi, pleased with her own pun. "It's those that's left behind I always feel sorry for, the dead are better off out of it!"

A hard stare from Aki silenced her.

"There, there, Youriko, there's nothing you can do from here. Let's have a glass of wine to your dear departed mother", she said filling the glasses. "Cheers!"

"Cheers!" they all toasted loudly except Youriko who just drank her chilled red wine and worked on how to drive the nail home.

Youriko seemed to recover as the wine went down and the girls started to tell the pick of the stories of their week after they had handed her their reports, which she put neatly into her handbag to peruse later that evening. Youriko always loved these meetings because they were excellent for moral and bonding, and just plain great fun. In fact, they were the only occasions when she got to enjoy herself in those days.

Six jugs of sangria later, the group prepared to split up or move on, Youriko wasn't sure which, but she wiped a tear from her eyes and her friends assumed that she was thinking about her parents again.

"Do you want me to stay with you a while, Youriko? I hate to leave you feeling down in the dumps like this while we're all going out, or why don't you change your mind and come with us?"

"No, it's all right, Aki", she replied, "I won't be good company now, and I'm feeling rather tired and a bit drunk anyway. Thanks for the offer though. You all go off and have a great evening. I'll see some of you tomorrow".

She made her way slowly and carefully down to her chalet, showered, put her dressing gown and the television on, swung her legs up onto the couch and started to read the first report. It was hard going. Between the television, the alcohol and the tiredness, she couldn't concentrate and had to reread some passages over and over again. It was a good job they'd eaten too or she'd be in a much worse state, she just didn't seem to be able to take a good session any more., after the camp.

She slept where she was for a few hours and then went to her room, but got up fully refreshed at six o'clock. She sat on the veranda with a bowl of cereal and tried the reports again. Then she took out the typewriter, put in a sheet of paper and set about collating the information into one report grouped by location not by team.

That is, she collated all the references into the report except one, the one that interested her the most. It was in the paperwork that Sasha had handed in and concerned a local man, named Yorgi, whom she had met while out with one of her friends. When he thought he was amongst only friends he had boasted about the money he made from smuggling overland to and from Turkey. The description was of a tall, broad man in his mid-thirties with black hair and a handlebar moustache. Yorgi was said to be very jovial, have a penchant for red wine and always to be telling stories and jokes. Sasha had met him twice with friends in a taverna called the 'Full Bottle' in Matsesta, a seaside resort fifteen kilometres along the coast to the south.

She decided that he was worthy of a personal investigation rather than passing him upstairs to her superiors.

She wouldn't have time that day, nor Saturday afternoon, because of the report and her meeting with her controller, but it seemed that Saturday night would be one of his nights out, so she wanted to try him then. Matsesta was not long by bus, only thirty or forty minutes and she could stay there the night if she had to or get a taxi back. She had a day and a half to think about it and possibly interview the girl who had met him.

It seemed like the best idea, so she rang Sasha and asked when she could talk with the girl. An appointment was made for that afternoon, and the girl, Mieke, would come to her.

As it happened, Mieke didn't have a lot more to tell, except that he looked as if he could be dangerous if he turned nasty, he carried a large knife, which he had used for peeling apples and possibly carried a gun, because she had noticed a bulge under his jacket 'like in the films'. She also said that despite his large size and the fact that he carried weapons, he was not intimidating and she liked him a lot, because he was good company.

Now, she just had to work out how to play the situation in the next twenty-four hours. She phoned Sasha again and asked her to ask Mieke if she could try to get her boyfriend to take her there on Saturday night, and if she did to say 'Hello' as if they were acquaintances from the resort. She should also ask Youriko to join them at their table.

There hadn't been a cultural problem with women going into bars on their own for decades, women's equality was far more advanced in the western half of the Soviet Union in that regard, so she didn't mind just going into the bar and waiting to see what happened, which is what she did. She sat at a table for two in a corner facing the door and order bread and cheese and a half carafe of local red wine, which she nibbled and sipped at while reading a book. The place was more than half empty at five fifteen, but nobody spoke to her.

A man she took to be Yorgi blocked the evening's feeble rays at just after six. He had to duck to get through the door. At about six foot six and four foot wide, he was a giant, with the gentle giant manner that is the story of legends. He was with two other men and seemed to be halfway through a hilarious yarn that had them in stitches. He called for something and was given a bottle of red wine and three glasses. She recognised it as the local tongue, but hadn't mastered it yet. When he noticed Youriko, he smiled, looked and pointed at her carafe and said in Russian,

"It is our wine, it is very good, eh?" and laughed out loud before turning back to his friends. She wondered who he thought she was: Russian, from one of the eastern Soviet republics or Oriental, but it didn't really matter he obviously knew that she wasn't local and probably just presumed that she was a holiday-maker.

She liked him; he was big enough to be honest and kind.

However, she didn't want to appear to be pushy or interested, so she kept reading her book and nibbling and sipping, until the barman surprised her.

"Excuse me, Miss, but the comrade wishes to buy you the 'second half of that bottle' as he puts it. Will you permit it?"

She looked up, but he was not watching, "Yes, please thank him".

The old carafe was emptied into her glass and refilled and some of the new wine was used to top up her glass. She held up her glass in toast and said a little louder than normal, "Cheers! Thank you, Comrade!" and "Good Health!" in his own language.

He held up his glass and repeated the toast, before returning to his friends. She went back to her book. At eight o'clock, it was time to either go for the last bus, or have another carafe and get a taxi later. She decided on the latter. At about nine fifteen, when Youriko was having difficulty focusing on the words in her book, a giggling young woman entered the bar backwards, obviously engaged with someone behind her.

"Stop it!" she implored giggling loudly some more, "Stop it! You know how ticklish I am by there. Spotting Yorgi, she begged, "Tell him to stop tickling me, Yorgi!"

"Where's he tickling you, Mieke? By here?" he asked joining in. She wriggled into the bar loving the attention, until she saw her boss. It was an automatic response, but it was too late, everyone had noticed and knew there was a connection. Mieke recovered quickly.

"What on Earth are you doing here, Youriko?" she asked loudly. "Everyone, this is my latest best friend from the resort, but I'm flabbergasted, what are you doing here?"

"Hi Mieke, I was just sightseeing and landed here, I was just about to get a taxi home".

"Oh, no, you can't do that, can she guys? Come and join us and Jimmy will take us back later, won't you, love?"

"Sure, what's everyone having?"

When they were about to leave at midnight, they were all shaking hands and kissing, Yorgi said, "Are you coming back tomorrow, Youriko?"

"Why?" she asked. "What's happening tomorrow?"

"Oh, nothing much, but some of us are going away on a little trip and we usually have a farewell do when someone leaves".

"Are you coming, Mieke?"

"Oh, I hope so. Are we, Jimmy?"

"Sure, it'll be fun. Do you want us to pick you up, Youriko? What time, Yorgi?"

"About two pm".

"How about one thirty, Youriko?"

"Sure, I'm looking forward to it. Thank you all for making me feel so welcome. See you all tomorrow".

If it hadn't have been for the wine, she wouldn't have slept a wink all night. She could feel in her bones that this had the making of an opportunity, but it would be difficult to play it right

They gathered at the 'Full Bottle' at two the next day and not many were even five minutes late. They sat at a long table opposite the bar, which was big enough to accommodate fourteen or sixteen people. Eventually, there were twenty-five. As the bread and cheese, wine and vodka went down, the talk became less guarded until there was no doubt in Youriko's mind that they were departing the following day on what seemed to be the work-week job of smuggling.

At one point, when Yorgi was not involved in the conversation, she leaned across the table and said in his ear, "Can I have a word with you in private, is there anywhere we can go to be alone?"

"This young woman wants to be alone with me!" he roared. "I'm a respectable married man, do I need a chaperon?"

She felt so embarrassed, but she smiled and shook her head.

"Tomas, can we use the back room for..."

"How long do you want me for, Youriko?" She held up five fingers. "Five hours?" he gasped, "I'll never last out! Oh, five minutes... for five minutes, Tomas?"

"Sure, it's open, but don't touch him Youriko, he prefers asses, er, in the sense of donkeys... unless I've been getting that arse about face all these years".

Everyone except Youriko was howling with laughter, but she was smiling broadly.

"Better top our glasses up if we're going to be in there five minutes," he said, standing up, then he opened the door for her.

"What is it, Youriko? Don't mind all that banter, what's on your mind?"

"Yorgi, I've only known you twenty-four hours, but I think I can be straight with you..."

"Keep going..."

"I have to get out of the USSR, you are a smuggler and I think you can help me do it".

"Wow! It doesn't come much straighter than that, does it? That's enough in one short sentence to get us both five to ten years".

"More for me, a lot, lot more, I've already tried once and did two years". She showed him some scars.

"But why should I admit to anything and risk the camps. You could be one of those agents provocateur".

"Yes, I could be, and I am in a way, I am KGB. Here's my warrant card".

Yorgi took the leather wallet and studied its contents. "Just been made sergeant, eh? I'm impressed."

She allowed him to think that she had just recently been promoted from corporal, and did not say that she had just joined the security forces.

"See, I'm being honest with you. I heard of you officially, but blocked the notification going up to my superiors, so that I could give you a chance to help me get out. If I had wanted you arrested, I could have done that last night when I got back".

"Why do you want to get out?"

"Love, just love of a man, nothing nefarious". Tears formed in her eyes and she sniffed. He rummaged in his pockets for a handkerchief, but he only had a dirty rag.

"Sorry", he apologised.

She smiled, sniffed again and wiped away her tears with her hands.

"Can you help me?"

"Well, I believe you, and I may be able to help, but I can't make any promises right now. We get back early on Saturday morning, can you be here at two again? We normally leave on a Monday morning".

"Thanks, Yorgi, though I can't get here until five, but I will be here for sure", she said stretching up to kiss him on the cheek as he opened the door. Everyone saw the kiss and howling and clapping erupted.

Yorgi shrugged his shoulders and allowed Youriko to enter first blushing deeply.

"It's just her way of saying 'Thank you', she's very polite like that", he said smiling as he sat down.

18 THE MULE TRAIN

She and Yorgi hadn't discussed anything. She didn't know whether the escape was on or off, or, if it was on, whether it was next week or the one after. It made trying to organise the operation a lot more difficult, because she could only complete minor tasks to facilitate her escape.

However, she had started to allow the rumour to spread that her father was depressed because her mother had died, by ringing her father every day from the bar, so that it would be noticed. The staff regularly asked after her father and she played up to them. She frequently ended such conversations with, phrases like: 'He needs me now, I feel so guilty sitting here' and 'I ought to go to him in his hour of need, I'm afraid he'll do something silly'.

She wrote him a letter, which she assumed would be opened by the KGB, in which she said that she would seek permission to go back to him for a holiday, and meanwhile, she worked like a Stakhanovite to pass the time more quickly until the Saturday when she could see Yorgi. When the day came, she took a taxi straight to the 'Bottle' after seeing her controller who, she noted, didn't mention the rumours about her going home, although that didn't mean anything. She knew that she couldn't trust him as far as she could throw him.

When the chance presented itself, she asked to speak to Yorgi in private. "Have you come to a decision about helping me?" she asked

"Sort of. I talked with my partners and they are willing to help, for a fee, but they don't want you to know any of the plan until they consider it necessary to reveal it to you".

"That's all right, how much?"

"They wanted five ounces of pure gold, but I persuaded them to accept three. Do you have that?"

"Who doesn't have three ounces of twenty-four carat gold lying around the house? Sorry. I'm not sure, Yorgi, to be honest. When would we be able to leave?"

"On Monday morning…"

"It doesn't give me much time to raise the gold does it?"

"You could wait until you do have it, if you like".

"No, no, I couldn't wait any longer, not now that I have a possible way out. That would be even worse than not having an escape plan at all! If I don't have all the gold, is there anything else they would accept?"

"Anything of value would do, but not the rouble, of course… What were you thinking of?"

"I don't know… I need to try to keep something back for when I get out. I don't want to be destitute when I get wherever I'm going. How about a book of fifty travel permits? I run a government team and some of them have to travel at short notice sometimes, so I have a book of travel vouchers…"

"That is a rare commodity indeed. Each voucher is worth at least a thousand roubles on the black market… I personally will give you an ounce of gold for that. It will come in very useful. Do you have the rubber stamp as well?"

"Of course, you can have that too… I meant the book and the stamp and the ink pad".

"I would have given you another ounce for the stamp, the pad and your KGB officer's ID number, if you had asked", he laughed. "How about your warrant card?"

"I wanted to keep that to prove that I am worth helping to defect in the West".

"Yes, I see, but I will give you another ounce for the stamp, the ink pad and your ID card number. I can't be fairer than that, can I? I can't steal from you, you're not very good at this negation lark, are you?"

"I suppose not", she smiled, "thank you, Yorgi".

"You are most welcome, Youriko, but you are paying a fair price, and we are not cheating you. It's nice to do business with you, my friend… Oh, before I forget. You said last week that you were Kazakh, right? So, I assume you have a Muslim background and can ride a horse?"

"I am Kazakh, and can ride a horse, but I am an atheist with a Muslim background from my grandparents. Why do you ask?"

"Oh, it's just that it may come in useful, that's all. I want you to go home tonight, at whatever time you like, but tomorrow, come back in the afternoon like last week and get very drunk, do not try to pretend, nearly all the people out there are my family and are professional drinkers, so if you try to act drunk they'll know and think something is going on. Anyway, my wife will join us in the evening and you will feel ill in the toilet, she will take pity on you and take you back to our house for the night so you can sleep it off. Make sure that you have made any arrangements you have to and that you have everything you need with you, because you will not be going back to your hotel again. When I say 'everything you need', I mean a small bag full, all right? Not everything you own

"Is that all clear? One more thing, write yourself a travel permit for Tbilisi". She nodded smiling broadly. "Good, let's rejoin the others then, but don't kiss me this time.

"Just a little business", he said to those assembled, "whose round is it?"

Youriko stayed until eight o'clock then made her excuses, promising to make a real session of it the next day when she had more time, and caught the bus back. It was just after nine when she arrived and she went straight to the bar.

"A double gin and tonic and the phone, please. I'm late phoning today, but Dad'll be awake, he has trouble sleeping," she said to the barmaid who listened politely, fetched her drink and then stood a short distance away. She drank her gin as she talked to her father and indicated another, she was hoping that the wine and gin mixture in her stomach would make her maudlin as she concentrated on the thought that she would never see her 'dear old Dad' again and that this might be the last time that she spoke to him. Tears ran down her cheeks as she said 'Goodbye' and hung up.

"How is your father tonight, comrade? Well, I hope".

"He fell down some stairs yesterday, sprained an ankle and broke a wrist. Things are going from bad to worse with him, I'm afraid, but thanks for asking. I'll have one more drink to help me sleep, then I'd better go, I'm not really in the mood to be sociable tonight. Put it all on my bill, please. Goodnight".

Youriko took her old book of travel permits, which still had seven in it, and cut out the next one and its yellow carbon copier tight to the binding with a razor blade, then she burned the copy, along with Sasha's report with the reference to Yorgi, and filled in the original permit with the designated destination as Tbilisi, then she stamped and signed it and put it in her bag. Next she stamped and signed the other six and filled out the last one with destination Alma Ata. She left the copy in place but took the original and put it in a purse. Then she put her new book of permits, the stamp and ink pad in her backpack, which she proceeded to fill with those items she considered essential and put that in a suitcase with other non-essential articles of clothing and the purse. She wrote her father's address on a piece of paper and affixed that to her case with sticky tape.

In the morning, she phoned Aki. "Hi, look, I need to see you tomorrow evening, if that's convenient. I've got this allergy and it has laid me up in bed. Don't worry it's not contagious, so I may be asleep or in the bathroom when you get here. To save a lot of messing about, I've told reception to give you a key to my room so you can let yourself in. Is that all right, darling? Sorry, I've got to go now I can feel my stomach rumbling – but it's the two-bob bits not hunger. See you, take care, Aki".

She spent a moment thinking how Aki had acquired her nickname and how it had stuck; she also spared a thought for other people that she would never see again and hoped that they would not suffer any retribution from the state if she were successful or indeed, even if she were not. She had no real evidence to go on, but she was an optimist, so she gave her defection a fifty-fifty percent chance of success.

"She wrote Aki a long, warm personal letter about their friendship and why she had to leave, but she substituted wanting to see her father in Kazakhstan for wanting to see Will in the UK. At the end of the letter, she added where the travel permits and the keys to the safe were, thanked Aki for her friendship in case anything went wrong, and begged her once again not to put herself in danger for her. She put that in an envelope addressed to Aki and left it on the bedside table.

Then she took her case up to breakfast at ten o'clock.

"Going anywhere nice, are we Youriko?"

"Pardon?" she replied, "Oh, the suitcase?" She looked embarrassed, "No, I'm just going to stay with some friends for a day or two". After breakfast, she gave her instructions regarding Aki to the receptionist and took a bus to the train station, where she bought a single ticket to Alma Ata. The train arrived punctually at one and she got on, chose a quiet carriage and sat down.

Once they were underway, she took her rucksack out of her case, put the case up in the rack, and went to the toilet, where she got changed, redid her make-up in a completely different style and put on a wig.

When the train stopped at the next station, she descended to the platform, and from there walked out onto the street, where she hailed a taxi to take her to the bus station in Matsesta, got changed again into her normal look in the toilets and walked along the beach to the "Bottle". As she entered the bar, she felt like Daniel walking into the lions' den, but she had burned her bridges and was now completely at their mercy.

She thought she put on a good performance at the bar, but she really was drunk when Trixy offered her a bed for the night. Youriko showered, thanked Trixy for her help and went to bed.

She was awoken at four thirty.

"Time to get up, Youriko", said Trixy outside the door banging it like a drum inside Youriko's head. She went down to meet them in the clothes she had worn the day before because she didn't have many changes of clothing.

"You look awful," said Yorgi eating a large cooked breakfast. "Perhaps you shouldn't drink so much", he added straight-faced but burst into laughter when Youriko stared at him in astonishment.

"Here's yours", said Trixy, "go on, eat it up, it'll do you good. Take these two aspirin as well, then a cup of strong tea and a shower and you'll be as right as rain".

Twenty-five minutes later, she felt able to say, "All right, that seems to have worked, I feel a lot better, what happens next?"

"Now you have to pay for your ticket".

"My ticket?" she queried.

"Just metaphorically speaking, but you still have to pay first".

"Half now and half later?"

"What's the point? Don't you think we don't know you have the money on you? We could just take it any time we liked and hand you over to the police for inciting us law-abiding citizens to help you escape to the West, couldn't we?"

"Now, don't be rotten, Yorgi, stop frightening the poor woman... but there are expenses to pay and people to satisfy that you do have the money, Youriko. Don't worry, you won't come to any harm, not if my Yorgi can help it, will she, love?" She placed a hand on his broad shoulder and he tapped it, smiling.

"I was only joking with you, Youriko, but you will have to trust us a lot, as we are trusting you. Did you know she's a KGB officer, Trixy?"

"What? I've had KGB sleeping under my roof? I never thought that day would come. Still, she's the nicest KGB officer I've ever met".

Youriko was digging in her bag and finally took out a pouch containing an ounce of pure gold in the form of eighteen and fourteen carat jewellery. In total, it weighed closer to forty-five grammes. Then she laid out the unused book of travel permits, the stamp, ink pad and her KGB identity card.

"You wanted to copy the ID number down, didn't you?"

"Yes, thanks", he said inspecting the book, the stamp and the card.

"I don't know anyone who's had a set of these before", he said with a certain amount of awe in his voice.

"No, nor me", agreed his wife.

"Do you need one of these?" he asked fanning the pages of the book.

"No, there were still a few pages in the old book".

"When do you think you'll be missed?"

She told him about the smokescreen she had set up.

"I'm no expert at this, but perhaps my controller won't miss me until Saturday, the conductor on the train might not realise something is up for a couple of days, but the hotel staff will miss me tomorrow, although they have no reason to find that suspicious or to report it. Realistically, I think it will be Wednesday, Thursday or possibly even Friday before alarm bells start ringing, but it's only a guess. When will I be out of the country?"

"About then, but we'd better get going now. Trixy, have you got a hat she can borrow? We want you to look a bit more masculine. Here, I borrowed this old jacket for you, put the hat on, and stick this cigarette in your mouth, you don't have to smoke it, but anyone seeing you through the window will think you're one of us.

"Let's hit the road". He kissed his wife goodbye and she and Youriko hugged.

"Good luck everyone. I hope you make it to the West to meet your man, Youriko… you're doing a terribly brave thing".

There were three others waiting for them in the yard, and all five were dressed like agricultural labourers, although Youriko's jeans looked too blue, too new, too tight and too clean. They got into the cab of Yorgi's old pickup and headed south out of town. The four men laughed, joked, cursed and coughed, but ignored her.

Once they were some kilometres out of town, Yorgi said, "You can forget the cigarette now, Youriko, but keep the hat on. We've got eight hours to Tbilisi, so if you want to sleep you can. If we're stopped we're going there for work and we're giving you, a friend, a lift so you can have a few days holiday. OK? You can take the jacket off as well, unless you're cold".

She wasn't cold, and was grateful to be allowed to sleep, although the atmosphere in the cab with all the smoke was poisonous, but if the windows were opened, too much dust came in. Youriko preferred the dust, but the others didn't, so she slept with the hat over her face as a makeshift filter. She looked like a small version of Clint Eastwood in one of the Spaghetti Westerns.

They arrived at a farm fifteen kilometres south-west of Tbilisi at just after five as the heat of the afternoon was starting to diminish. They had not been stopped, but then they rarely were because they knew where the checkpoints were and how to avoid them. Youriko was shown to a room above a barn, which they described as a guest room, and told to stay there until Yorgi came back for her in twenty-four hours.

He said that they had business in Tbilisi and it was safer for her to stay there. It was comfortable and they brought her plenty of hearty food and wine, so she didn't really mind. It was just dull. There was nothing to do. She had forgotten to bring a book, but she drank red wine and contemplated the countryside and her future and the time passed, but it was a day and a half before Yorgi reappeared in her doorway.

"I'm sorry we're a bit late, were you worried?"

"Sometimes, but not much. I'm sure you won't let me down, your wife has too much faith in you for you to disappoint her. It is quite obvious that you love each other very much".

"Yes, well, come on down for breakfast and then were off for a drive again. Have you ever been to Georgia before? No? Well, you're getting to see a lot of it now, with plenty more to come"

After an early breakfast, they drove the two hundred kilometres west-south-west to a farm outside Samtskhe-Javakheti It wasn't that far, but it took them six hours because of the quality of the minor roads they used.

"Wow!" was the first word that escaped her lips when they drove over the crest of a hill and Yorgi explained that their destination was the farm ahead of them. "I haven't seen that many horses since I left home! There're hundreds of them!"

"Yes, it's a beautiful sight, they're not all horses though, there are donkeys, mules and all sorts as well. Let's take a closer look".

The owner and his family treated Yorgi and the other three men, who may have been his family, just like family, and for all Youriko knew they were related. There was lots of back-slapping and hugging, and food and drink was brought out in large quantities.

"Are we staying here tonight, Yorgi?" asked Youriko.

"Oh, yes, it would be terribly rude to decline the feast that they'll be putting on for us. Why, are you not happy here?"

"Happy here? Yes, it has a good atmosphere, but I'm not really sure where 'here' is".

"Good", he replied, "it's a lot safer that way. You'll have a better idea tomorrow or the day after, but for tonight, just enjoy yourself, because we leave at first light".

She did too and so did all the others, about thirty in all including the farmer's family and the leading farm hands both male and female. They ate, danced, sang and drank until midnight, when Youriko was offered a space on the floor in the house or a place in a barn, but she chose to sleep nearby, under the stars for the first time since she had been camping in school with the Komsomol, the communist youth organisation, which was similar to The Scouts in the West.

"Breakfast, cowboys and cowgirls!" shouted Yorgi at five thirty. If you don't eat now, you don't eat until lunch!"

Breakfast included wine. Youriko felt compelled by the laws of hospitality to drink two glasses with her hearty meal, but the rest of her friends from Sochi drank a bottle or more each.

"What's the plan for today, Yorgi?"

"I'm sorry, Youriko, but I don't want to tell you, you'll find out soon enough, but, please, don't worry, trust me, it is not going to be bad".

"I trust you, like I said, it's just a natural curiosity".

They took their leave of their hosts, and one of their team jumped into the station wagon and drove off. Youriko was a little confused.

"I thought we were all leaving, Yorgi?"

"Yes, we are, Kazakh, mount up, we have fifty-five assorted donkeys and mules to deliver way over yonder. Have you ever driven a herd of mules before?"

"No, but I'm looking forward to trying?! Which mount is mine?"

Yorgi spoke to a man: "Any one you fancy".

She looked as excited as a child at Christmas. She walked down the line of six tethered horses and spoke to each one privately, patting its head and breathing on its nose. After ten minutes, during which the others looked on fascinated because Kazakhs were legendary throughout the Soviet Union as fantastic horsemen and women:

"I'll take this one," she said swinging up into the saddle, what are you all waiting for?" She leaned over the horse's head, patting it and nuzzling her own head to it

"Whohoo!" shouted Yorgi and led the race to the horses. Soon they were all mounted and the donkeys were released tied to one another in a line.

"Wagons roll!" shouted Yorgi in jest for Youriko's sake and they began their slow procession out of the farm.

She had never herded animals from horseback before, although she had herded sheep on foot, but it seemed that her horse had, so she just applied common sense and watched her more experienced colleagues for direction. Most of the work seemed to be tapping an animal on the rear from time to time with a stick to hurry them along, which really just meant walk. The lead donkeys had been trained as pack animals, but all the animals carried something, though not much. Youriko was dying to know what was in the packs, but thought it prudent not to ask. Eventually, a question did pop out, she couldn't help it, she was naturally curious.

"What's going to happen to these animals?" she asked.

"Happen? What do you mean 'happen'?" he asked. "I'm not sure. We just bought them from one farmer, who buys and breeds them, now we are delivering them to a dealer, who will do what he wants with them. We make this trip four times a year. The donkeys are perfectly legitimate, and as far as I know, this man will sell them on in Turkey, Greece and the surrounding area as working farm animals or as rides in the tourist industry. Why?"

"I'm just curious. How long will we be doing this?"

"I not going to tell you, but you will find out soon enough".

Ten hours later, which was eight hours in the saddle except for lunch, which was spent mostly feeding the animals, they turned into another farm near Akhaltsikhe, where they were also well known, and the animals were corralled and fed and the humans were treated to another feast.

In the morning, they set off again, but after five hours, Yorgi rode up to Youriko.

"Are you saddle sore yet, Kazakh? You haven't done this much riding this in a long while, have you?"

"No, that's true, and my behind is a little bit sore, but I'm loving being in the saddle again. I wouldn't have missed it for anything".

"Oh, in that case, I'm not sure whether I have good news for you or not, but I wanted to be the first to congratulate you, Youriko, you are now a free woman in the province of Ardahan, in the country of Turkey".

They were both beaming from ear to ear and leaned over in the saddle to embrace, tears streaming down Youriko's face.

"I can't believe it, no, I do believe it, it feels right, but it is such a relief... Er, what happens now?"

"That's easy, we have to deliver these animals to a farm ten kilometres west of here, then we have a big party, then you go somewhere and we go home in the car".

"But I don't understand, don't you get any hassle from customs, ours or the Turkish ones, for crossing borders like this?"

"We used to, but now they trust us and we pay them enough. We're not interested in leaving our homeland and they know that now. The borders between countries don't bother us, we always pay and we always go back. We are good for the local economy and we make a little extra for ourselves at the same time. What is so wrong with that? They are practical people and so are we. They know that we can avoid them and then they'll get nothing, but if we pay, we get a more direct route, so we pay and they look in the other direction. That way, everyone's happy and then we go home, so no-one gets into trouble..

"So, my friend Youriko, for I think of you as such, what do you want to do now? That is the question, do you want to come with us for one last party, or do you want to head off into the sunset and begin your search for that very lucky man, who is the love of your life?"

"We have waited for each other for over a year, I think one more party won't hurt, do you, my friend?"

"I was hoping you'd say that, follow me".

Andropov's Cuckoo

19 THE LAST LEG

The morning after the party on a farm in the area known as Posof, in eastern Turkey, Youriko, Yorgi and the owner of the farm sat talking over a bottle of wine in the late morning. The two men spoke together almost fluently, laughing and joking like old friends. However, Youriko could only understand the odd word and phrase, and that only because her native tongue was also Turkic. Yorgi was now asking about the best way of getting to a British Embassy, which Youriko had said was her ultimate destination in Turkey.

"He says he doesn't even know if there is a British Embassy in Turkey, but that is obviously nonsense. Wait a minute". He spoke to the farmer again, "How far is it to Ankara, old friend?"

"Ankara? Oh, a very long way, far too far for me… I've never been there, and never will do now either. My eldest son's been there though. He went for his honeymoon… took his wife as well, you know?" he chuckled at his own joke. "It took him sixteen hours on the bus! Each way that is, to think that he wasted three working days just travelling, not even being on holiday! I think he said it was about eleven hundred kilometres… I think that's too far to go just for a holiday myself, but young people don't think like us older ones… They've got to see everything and try everything… Heaven knows why, but I don't.

"No, I'm sorry, I can't help on that score, but I'll have them look for my son if you like and you can ask him yourself".

"No, it's all right for now, old friend, perhaps we'll speak to him later".

"It looks like you're going to have to get to Ankara, Youriko, which is about eleven hundred kilometres away. Have you got enough money for that?"

"I've no idea, but I haven't actually got any cash at all. I have some gold left and two watches, but they are very nice ladies' watches… very dainty and very sparkly".

Yorgi spoke to the old man again.

"He says he'll give you ninety thousand lira an ounce for the gold".

"I have no idea what that means, Yorgi, is that fair? Is it enough to do what I need to do? It's all I've got left in the world".

"There's no doubt that it is a lot of money, Youriko, a farm labourer might get four hundred lira a day. If you said four fifty, it's worth three months' work. It will be enough to get you to Ankara easily, but let me see what I can do".

They spoke again, raised their voices and slapped their thighs, chuckled and swore. Then they clinked glasses and looked at Youriko, who realised that she had to do something but wasn't sure what. She touched glasses with the men and drained her glass like they did.

"What happened there?" she asked.

"I reminded him that the lira was losing value every second that we wasted haggling and that he ought to be trying to help a good Muslim woman escape oppression by the Soviet atheists".

"He asked where your headscarf was, if you were such a devout Muslim, and I said you'd had to discard it on the trail because you were posing as a male drover. Under those circumstances, he is prepared to offer you twelve hundred dollars for the gold and ninety lira per dollar. You would probably get five thousand lira more in an assay office, if you had a passport, so I think you ought to take it and thank him".

She did just that. She also thanked Yorgi.

"Good, now give him the gold".

The old man shuffled off and returned with a box, from which he extracted a set of scales and a magnifying glass, then closed it again. He proceeded to check the assay marks on the various pieces and their purity, which was eighteen carat for all of them, and finally weighed them collectively. Thirty-six grammes, a little over. Next, he took a bundle of money from the box and started to count out a pile onto the low table between them. He stopped at ninety thousand and looked around, gave a wicked laugh and carried on to a hundred and eight thousand, which he handed to her with both hands, then put the gold in his box, locked it and hid it under a pillow by his side.

He spoke to Yorgi again and shouted something over his shoulder.

"He says he is happy to do business with you and he wants to restore your modesty with one of his daughters' headscarves".

A young woman entered the room and looked at the old man, he indicated Youriko with a glance, and she handed a beautifully-embroidered headscarf to Youriko. She hadn't worn one since dressing up as a peasant for a play in school, but she put it on and thanked him again. The old man looked at the money she had put back on the table to tie the headscarf and pushed it towards her. He obviously didn't like to see large sums of cash lying about, so she put it in her bag.

The old man spoke again and Yorgi leaned, took both his hands and shook them warmly.

"He says he will tell his son to drive you to Ardahan free of charge and put you on the overnight bus to Ankara to make sure that you start the next leg of your long journey safely. They will do this free of charge because of our long-standing friendship and because he would not like to see any harm come to such a brave young woman. He says that if he were twenty years younger, he would ask you to become one of his wives, but there is no point now".

She looked at the old man and smiled, but he could only guess what was being said, because he didn't speak Russian.

"It's about ninety minutes to Ardahan", continued Yorgi "and the bus departs at six, so you should arrive just before noon tomorrow. He suggests that if the police stop you, and there is a fair chance that they will, that you don't say you're Russian, but rather that you are a British Muslim on holiday going to the embassy for repatriation because all your documents have been stolen. It is dangerous for a woman to travel alone here, even a Turkish Muslim woman, but if you stay on the bus and pretend to be British, you should be all right.

"Do not even try to speak any language but English or they may suspect something".

At four o'clock an old car was brought around and there was much handshaking and hugging among the Russians. Youriko cried and took off her wristwatch.

"I want you to give this to Trixy for me. It's not much, but she was so kind to me, you both were".

The big man leaned down, but his hand on her shoulders and kissed her on the cheek. "That is to say 'thank you' for the watch from Trixy, and this", he kissed her again, "is to say that I am pleased that we met and doubly pleased that I have played some part in your escape to join the love of your life. Have a safe journey, my friend… and what did you say that Andropov called you, his Little Cuckoo? He was wrong, you are no-one's Little Cuckoo, you soar like an Eagle!"

She hugged him again, and the tears flowed again as well. It was the kindest thing that anyone had said to her for many years.

As she moved towards the car, the old man's eldest son's wife opened the front passenger door with a degree of show and got in, so Youriko opened the back door behind her. "Yorgi?" she said, "I have to ask. What did we bring through in those saddlebags?"

He laughed, "I knew it was still bothering you! DIY beehives, it's a thriving industry around here. I told you before we are basically honest traders, who do some private business as well. That's why we can come and go, the patrols trust us… and we give them a little money to buy their sweethearts presents".

"Thanks", she smiled and got into the car, then it took off in a cloud of dust.

Nobody spoke to her during the car ride, perhaps they couldn't be bothered to try, but Youriko got the feeling that the driver's wife was there because she was not going to allow her husband to be alone with a Russian woman for two hours and so had decided to accompany them, although it may just have been that going to the big city was an occasion that she could talk about for the next week. Either way, Youriko was glad she was there, just in case he had got ideas that would have been awkward.

The couple helped her buy her ticket and found her somewhere quiet to wait, from where she could see the bus come in. As they were about to leave, Youriko took off the other watch she had put on in the car and gave it to the woman. She looked at it as if it was the most valuable item she had ever held, and it could well have been. She spoke to her husband and sat down. He returned shortly with three bottles of water and they waited for the bus together in silence, but it must have seemed like an awfully long time coming to the wife because she was checking the time every few minutes.

She was glad to get on the bus when it arrived. The last few days had been stressful rather than tiring and she was glad that Yorgi hadn't told her more about their plans, because she might have gone to pieces when they were near and then actually crossing the border. It made her wonder whether he had helped people escape before, but he was difficult to read because he always seemed to have just heard the funniest joke in the world. She liked him, and his wife, and his mates or family or whatever they were.

She knew that she would sleep a lot of the coming sixteen hours especially when it was dark, which it was starting to get as the bus pulled away from its stop and she waved goodbye to her new friends. She was already thinking about how she would handle an encounter with the police should they make a spot check of the bus, which they frequently did in the USSR, so she assumed they might also do in Turkey.

She was awoken by a tap on the shoulder.

"Miss, it's eleven o'clock, we are stopping for fuel and food. It will be the last stop for seven hours, do you want to disembark to eat something?" the stewardess on the VIP coach asked in English.

She decided to heed the old man's advice, "No, thank you, I am too tired to eat". There was a toilet on the bus, so she didn't need to get off for that and she still had half a bottle of water, so she went back to sleep.

The same occurred at six am.

"Miss, this is our last scheduled stop before Ankara, would you like to disembark for breakfast or to stretch your legs?"

"No, thank you, I have already come a long way and would rather just sleep".

The bright sunlight streaming in through the tinted windows awoke her again at a little past ten and she assumed that the sprawl of buildings on either side of the motorway was part of the city's suburbs. She sat up and ran through her answers to all the questions she thought they might ask her. There were two, or at the absolute worst, three groups of people who might interview her: the British Embassy security staff, the Turkish police force and the Russian security services attached to the Soviet Embassy, if she were handed over to them. Whoever she had to talk to, whatever Fate had in store for her, she decided to just tell the truth and hope for the best. The basis of her story was simply that she was in love with a British guy and didn't want to live without him.

When she got off the bus, she had to shield her eyes from the glare of the blazing midday sun, but there were taxi drivers all around her. Some tried Turkish, others English.

"I know good hotel, Miss, first class very, very cheap!" She didn't want one of the pushy noisy ones, so she moved forward and they parted before her like the frozen sea before an icebreaker. They knew better than to molest a Muslim woman in broad daylight.

"Do you speak English?" she asked a young man who caught her eye.

"Little bit", he replied.

"Good", she smiled, "you know the British Embassy? Is it a long way?"

"I know, not long."

"How much?"

"I not sure, but I have a taxi meter".

"OK, we go," she said getting in. She laughed later about asking whether it was far. She had to get there anyway and had plenty of money to pay the fare whatever it was, but she was so used to getting some information from taxi drivers before she accepted a ride that it had been automatic.

She walked past the Turkish security guards on the gate with a happy smile into the main building, but she didn't know what to do next, so she took a brochure from a stand and sat down. She looked at the row of girls behind glass like tellers in a bank, but the reasons for taking a number to see one of them did not include defection. It wasn't one of the options on the long list of reasons hanging from the ceiling for having to go upstairs either. After fifteen minutes, she decided to ask, before someone came to ask what she was doing there.

She considered that the closest option she could see to what she wanted was a visa, so she took a ticket and resumed her seat. She was sure, that the girl she would get to see would not be able to help, but at least she had a legitimate reason for sitting there now, and something would come of it, but what?

She had no idea. Even her experience from the Japanese Embassy didn't help. She had never met anyone who had wanted to deflect to Japan in all the time she was there.

While she was daydreaming, deep in thought, she heard her number being called out and saw it flashing on a screen. She stepped up to the glass and spoke through the baffled hole.

"Hello..."

"Good afternoon, Miss. How may I help you?"

"This is going to sound odd, I know it will, but I escaped from the Soviet Union two days ago and would like to apply for asylum in the United Kingdom".

The girl looked up and studied her face.

"So you're not British?"

"No, I am a Soviet citizen", she replied, but she was thinking, 'I wouldn't be seeking asylum if I were British, would, I?"

"I see, please stay there while I get someone who can help you".

Those words frightened her, because that was what a Soviet apparatchik would say before sending for the police. This girl went to talk to her supervisor, but Youriko didn't know that. As the girl retook her seat with Youriko concentrating on her, a man touched her shoulder. She jumped and yelped as if his hand had been a cattle prod.

"I'm terribly sorry for startling you, Miss, er..."

"Myrskii", she helped.

"Miss Myrskii, will you come with me to my office, please?"

She followed him and sat where he indicated.

"Wait a few moments, I'll have some refreshments sent in before we start. When they had arrived, the First Secretary started a tape recorder and date stamped it with his voice, then he asked Youriko to identify herself and tell her story.

"From where, sir?" she asked.

"From wherever you think it is relevant", he replied.

She told him her life story starting from the days that her mother began hosting secret CPJ parties, through the amazing switch of identities and her life in Bonn, to her failed escape bid in Canada and everything that transpired after that right up to her flight from the Krasnodarskaya Krai that very week.

He, Mr. Jenkins, did not give his feelings away in the slightest, but asked whether she could corroborate her story.

"I don't have much, they didn't give me my possessions back when I left the camp", she said sarcastically, and regretted it immediately, "but I do have a few things. Here is my travel permit signed by myself and my KGB sergeant's warrant card. Oh, and they gave me a fake Japanese identity card so that I could pose as a student from there. See?" she asked handing everything over.

He called his secretary over the intercom and asked her to photocopy the things she had given him.

"Is there anything else you can give me?"

She showed him her scars, but knew that they could have come from a vicious lover or a motor accident. You could contact the Japanese Foreign Office and check my photo", she watched him write that down, "and you could phone the real Yui..."

"The one in Toronto?" he asked.

"Yes, and you could contact my boyfriend in the UK... but that's about it".

"Yes, well, Miss, er what should I call you?"

"Officially, I am Natalya Petrovna Myrskii, but you may call me Youriko, in remembrance of Operation Youriko, which got me and so many others into trouble and was eventually responsible for killing my mother and wrecking our family. It is what William calls me too. But Comrade Yuri Vladimirovich Andropov used to call me Natasha, or his Little Cuckoo, before he had me slung into a penal camp. Choose the company you'd like to be associated with".

"Yes, well, I will call you Youriko then, if it's all the same to you. Now all this information will have to be processed and verified. What are your immediate plans while that is taking place?"

She looked at him as if he were from another planet.

"I was smuggled into Turkey about thirty-six hours ago, I know no-one and have no passport. Therefore, I cannot go to a hotel and I cannot risk being picked up by the police in case they deport me or hand me over to the KGB. In both cases, I would be sent back to the Gulag and die! I don't have any plans, I was hoping you would help me".

"Yes, I see. Well, one thing is certain, we cannot issue you with any travel documents or identity papers because you are not British. I will have to talk to my fellow officers. Please wait here. Would you like more tea? This pot went cold some time ago?"

She asked for more and he left. The tension was bad, this was make or break, she didn't think she had any chance of surviving more than a night or two on the streets without being arrested for not having valid papers. If that happened, she thought she would have at least a fifty percent chance of being deported to Georgia and handed over to the authorities, which would mean the camps again.

Mr. Jenkins returned twenty-five minutes later apologising profusely for having kept her waiting.

"The fact is", he began slowly, "it puts us in the embassy in a tricky situation. We are now harbouring an illegal immigrant, who has insufficient documentation to support her case. However, your situation is not without precedent, Youriko, I am happy to say. We can't just turn you out whilst we investigate your story in case you disappear back into the Soviet Union, where you will face certain imprisonment and probably torture. If that didn't happen, you would probably finish up in a Turkish prison for not having any papers and that is something we wouldn't want on our conscience either.

"Therefore, the Ambassador has suggested offering you one of the rooms we keep here on the premises for visiting dignitaries from back home. Would that be acceptable, until we can verify what you have told me?"

She wanted to hug and kiss him.

"Oh, yes! Yes! My story will stand up. Then what, Mr. Jenkins? You have given me more hope than I have had for several years".

"I'm afraid that a lot of work will have to be done between now and 'then', Youriko, so let's just take it one step at a time for now. However, I would like to congratulate you for getting this far. It is a remarkable achievement. Now, I must start work on your case, so I will send a female aide to take you to your room and discuss any needs you may have.

"I take it that that bag is all the luggage you have brought? Yes, well talk to the aide about that as well. I may see you tonight or otherwise tomorrow. One thing though, please don't try to contact the telephone numbers of the people you have given me until I have spoken to them first. In any case, the switchboard will not connect you. Goodbye for now".

The aide took her to a small, but very nice room with a window onto the rear garden.

"How are you off for clothes, Youriko?"

"I have three sets, all dirty, but I am wearing the best of them. Is there a chance of getting new? I have money".

"We can send out for basic things for you: T-shirts, tops, shorts, skirts, jeans, knickers and bras, but God knows what colours or styles you'll end up with. If you give me your measurements, I'll send a girl out. Anything else?"

"A dressing gown?"

"Behind the wardrobe door, you'll find slippers in there as well. All guests receive them. Toiletries? Make-up?"

"I'm not to bothered for now, just perfume, shampoo and soap..."

"Shampoo and soap are complementary, as are towels. Which perfume? And anything else?"

"Anything that doesn't smell of horses or mules... and some food, I haven't eaten today".

"No problem, you can either eat with us in the embassy restaurant, or you can order a meal to be delivered to your room. That is before nine am and from six till ten pm only. The phone and the menu are on the table over there. I'll see you later. It's nice to have you with us, you're the talk of the embassy today, you know! I'll see you later... relax, you're safe now".

Youriko felt that she owed it to the embassy staff not to just stay in her room, although that was her preferred option. Instead, she showered for a long time and put the dressing gown on. If clothes, any clean clothes at all came back before eight, she would join them, otherwise she would eat in her room, but she couldn't bring herself to sit with them in clothes that she had been riding and travelling in for four days. Her other things smelled even worse, she realised, of damp.

The girl she had met before, Gail, brought an assortment of clothing up to her at seven thirty.

"How much do I owe you?" she asked.

"Not me", replied Alice in a jocular tone, "pay the boss when he asks for it. Are you coming down to join us later?"

"Well, I'd love to but, you know in this gear, and I don't know anyone..."

"You know me! I'll come by and collect you at eight. All right? Deal? We'll go together".

After the British government had arranged for her to have a pink 'Stateless' passport and a six-month visa to the UK, sometimes, Gail was able to take her out in Ankara and show her the sights or take her to a restaurant and they became good friends. They vowed that they would keep in touch when the time came for Youriko to leave.

The night before her departure, the embassy staff threw a party in her honour. She had never seen so many feasts and parties in one week in all her life. It seemed to auger well for her future, or that's how she decided to interpret it, and the day after, the Ambassador had her driven to the airport in his limousine and she was flown to the UK first class at the taxpayers expense. It just kept getting better and better and she dared to fantasise that she would be in William's arms within a day or so.

It made for a peaceful night's sleep and very pleasant dreams.

Andropov's Cuckoo

20 CHELTENHAM

She was met off the plane at Heathrow by a male and a female MI5 officer and taken to a holding area where her identity was established by checking her documents and telephoning Mr. Jenkins, who was Secret Intelligence Service, better known as MI6, for a brief physical description of her. Then she was asked to sign the Official Secrets Act. None of this bothered her at all, she had been expecting it.

However, if Youriko thought that gaining admission to the UK meant that she would be able to come and go as she pleased or hook up with Will right away, she was very much mistaken. She was kept in a facility, a very comfortable facility though it was, at the Government Communications Headquarters, commonly known as GCHQ in Cheltenham. You may be forgiven for thinking that it is a giant telephone exchange from its name, but it is, in fact, the main unit in the British intelligence and security organisation, responsible for providing signals intelligence and information assurance to the British government and the armed forces.

It operates under the formal direction of the Joint Intelligence Committee (JIC) along with the Security Service (MI5), the Secret Intelligence Service (MI6) and Defence Intelligence (DI). Ultimately and formally, it is the responsibility of the UK Secretary of State for Foreign and Commonwealth Affairs, but it is not a part of the Foreign Office.

It is also one of the places where they debrief defectors and criminal terrorists. The latter would be kept in cells similar to any prison, but defectors like Youriko are accommodated in the sort of luxury associated with a four or five star hotel, but without the automatic ability to communicate with the outside world.

Mr. Jenkins at Ankara had implied that he had carried out all the verification of Youriko's story himself, but he had merely passed the details on to GCHQ, which had assigned officers to study the case. They had contacted Chou and William Davies, ascertained that they knew her and under what circumstances, and assured them that she was safe in the West, but was incommunicado pending the completion of her debriefing.

She stayed within the complex at Cheltenham for ten days, but it was under her own free will, as they told her, they would deport her back to the Soviet Union any time she asked to go. However, although that was not an option to her, she really quite liked assisting the security services, of what she hoped would become her new home, with their enquiries. It soon became clear that she was a low-level officer in the KGB, but she was able to tell them about life in the corrective labour camp she knew and they showed her thousands of photographs of other dissidents in the hope that she had met some of them, although she hadn't.

However, she was able to tell them about the hotel in North Korea that the CPJ had used and which could still be an underground route into the Soviet Union for all she knew. They didn't say so, but she was pretty sure that that piece of information was news to them. They also seemed to be interested in the layout of the part of the Lubyanka that she had seen and drew several sketches and floor plans of it. They also compared her knowledge with that of other people and questioned her relentlessly on what parts of it were true and what might have been made up just to satisfy the interrogators or even to throw them off the scent.

She honestly tried to be as useful as she could and they seemed satisfied with what she had to offer. On a lighter note, they seemed to find it fascinating that Andropov would take such a personal interest in a girl and her mother, but she explained that her mother was considered a high-flier in the local Communist Party of Alma Ata and almost certainly had an affair with him when she had to go to Moscow to discuss the switch, which was code-named Operation Youriko, from where she had taken her latest name.

Despite everything he had done to her or had had done to her, she admitted to having a soft spot for him, because he had been personally responsible for releasing her from the Gulag system three years early, getting her a 'decent job' with responsibility and giving her her money back, by doing which he had unwittingly provided her with the wherewithal to buy the gold to get out of the country. She felt that she owed everything that she had to look forward to to Andropov. They were interested in Andropov's character, and she felt that they too considered him to be a front-runner as a replacement for the ageing and now often sick Leonid Brezhnev.

She was also finally able to break the promise she had made not to tell anyone about the true nature of her job of the previous two years. She got the impression that they knew that such honey-pot traps existed, but she also thought that she added to their information, because they were interested in how carefully the operation was orchestrated. It seemed to surprise them that there were organised teams of young women targeting businessmen, students and tourists of all nationalities, even Soviet.

When the security services at GCHQ had finished with her, they asked whether she would be willing to assist them at any time they deemed it necessary in the future, which she also agreed to. They allowed her to stay one more night in 'their hotel', installed a telephone for her and provided her with forms to apply for British citizenship, which they assured her would be granted. They also gave her five thousand pounds and a contact name and number, which she was told she had to ring every day so that they knew where she was and if she was all right.

The first thing she did was telephone Chou.

"Guess who?" she asked when she heard her friend's voice, "I'm out!"

"Oh, my God! Really? Some woman with a British accent, police, I think, phoned me about two weeks ago and said that you were being held in Turkey for processing, but that you were all right. She wouldn't say much more, but she didn't sound very hopeful. She was more interested in how I knew you. I didn't know how much to tell them about the swap, you know… I didn't know who they were, they could have been Russian for all I knew. Anyway, I think she realised I was being cagey, because a couple of hours later, I had the Canadian Security Intelligence Service waiting for me at my flat… anyway, never mind about that now, I'll tell you all about it when I see you.

"Where are you? In Canada? How are you? I've been so worried!"

"Slow down. First, I'm sorry to have caused you so much worry, it must have been awful for you. Second, I'm fine. They actually have been looking after me very well, first in the British Embassy in Turkey where I handed myself over, and then in the UK where they have been debriefing me. They're letting me out tomorrow, isn't that great?"

"What! They've had you in jail?"

"No, not in jail, in a sort of safe house, where their guys could talk to me whenever they wanted to… It was very nice".

"So, what now, are you coming over here?"

"No, there's a man over here…"

"A man? You? I'm sorry, but I've never heard you talk about men ever since I met you. Who is he?"

"I didn't really have time for men back then… Anyway, this man's name is William and he's studying Russian in the UK".

"Studying? You don't mean teaching?"

"No, but he is in his final year!" she laughed.

"You are a dark horse, aren't you? You don't bother with men all your life and then fall in love with a toy boy… I envy you. So, what now? Can I come over there?"

"I was hoping you would. I'm sort of on my own…"

"OK, I'll fly into Heathrow tomorrow, can you meet me there if I phone you back with the details?"

"Sure, that'd be great, Chou, I'll see you tomorrow. Bye, sister".

She hung up and cried. She hadn't used the word 'sister' for so long, but it still felt right, it had just tripped off her lips.

One of the girls who had been looking after her at GCHQ booked a bus ticket for Youriko and Gail took her to the station in the morning to catch it. She was in Heathrow Airport shortly after noon and made her way to the arrival gate for Chou's flight. She was an hour early so she had a coffee and a toasty in a shop where she could keep an eye on the arrivals and departures board.

She spotted Chou immediately. She was wearing a half-length fur coat, a fur hat and thigh-high black leather boots and dragging a medium-sized suitcase on wheels. Youriko had on two T-shirts, two jumpers and jeans and was feeling the cold a little, it being early October.

"You look like a film star, Chou! You really look fantastic, sister!"

"And you look a bit like a street urchin, sis, come here and give me a hug".

They embraced and had tears in their eyes until Chou took charge of the situation. "Come on, we don't want to stand here all day, let's get to a hotel and have a long chat over lunch and a bottle of wine".

They took a taxi to the Heathrow Hilton and booked a twin room.

"I usually stay here a night before moving on", she explained, "it's convenient. So where are we going to move on to? No, don't tell me, let's get down to the restaurant and make ourselves comfortable first, then you can tell me everything that's been going on in your life and especially about this William guy!"

"Mine is a long story, Chou, do you mind telling me about the Canadian Special Branch first, I need to know what they said".

"Oh, all right. Well, like I said yesterday, I was pretty worried what they'd do about me. I was an illegal, after all, so I ummed and ahhed, but then thought, sod it, what's the worst they can do? Deport me to Japan? If that happened I'd still be rich and I'd just deny all knowledge of the switch. I would just say I couldn't take the job any more. and left, that's all I know.

"Anyway, so, I just told them that I've known you for twelve years, last saw you in Japan, but knew you were working in the Japanese Embassy in Bonn. Then I told them that one morning, the last time I saw you, while heading to the police station so you could defect, I got clobbered and you were abducted, presumably by KGB stationed in Canada.

"They thanked me and that was the last I saw of them. It was scary at the time, but looking back on it, it was no big deal. OK, your turn, I'm dying to hear this".

They had finished their meal and were on the second bottle of wine by the time Youriko had finished.

"That's the most gruesome tale, yet most romantic story I've ever heard! Oh, come here, sis, let me give you a big hug, you poor woman!"

"Yes, the end might have seemed romantic, Chou, but being in jail and the camp wasn't. I thought they'd knocked all the romance out of me up there, but from the moment I saw Will, I couldn't take my eyes off him…" Tears trickled down her cheeks again.

"There, there, sis, all those bad days are behind you now. So what do you want to do tomorrow? Go look for him?"

"Yes, he's at a place called Southampton. I've seen it on the map, it's not far south-west of here about a hundred kilometres. Oh! I should be talking miles now, shouldn't I? About sixty miles, I think… two hours on the bus anyway".

"Nothing in the UK is far for us, sis. I've just come about three and a half thousand miles and you about… I don't know, but a long way…"

"Three and a half thousand kilometres".

"There you go then, so what's a piddly, little sixty miles more? We'll head down there tomorrow, but today is only for us. It has been so long, nearly five years and you saw him only a few months ago. I want you all to myself, because I can tell that I won't get a look in when you're with William".

Youriko blushed and vowed to herself to try to strike the right balance when the three of them were together.

The following morning, they caught the ten am coach for Southampton, which got them in at noon. They took a taxi to the Southampton Hilton Hotel on the advice of the driver, where Chou suggested they get separate rooms 'for obvious reasons'. Youriko blushed again.

"It's my turn to pay for the rooms this time, Chou, I can't let you go on paying for everything".

"It's very sweet of you, sis, but I've probably got enough money to fill that little rucksack of yours with gold and all you've got in there are a few cheap clothes from the market. I am not trying to be funny or nasty, but the bra and knickers set I'm wearing right now probably cost more than all your things put together, and I have you to thank for all that. You have had a few rough breaks and as your soul sister, I want to help you get on your feet. You can understand that, can't you? I know you'd do the same for me if the situations were reversed". Youriko said nothing. "So, let's hear no more about it, and you haven't even got a job or a work permit and you're going out with a poverty-stricken student!"

"We'll have to do something about that later…" Youriko was about to speak, when Chou continued. "I don't mean about your boyfriend, I mean about your wardrobe".

Youriko grinned with relief.

"Come on then, dear, I know you're itching to see him and whatever, so put that jacket I gave you on, and let's go find him".

They walked the mile to the Humanities Department of the university because it was a warm afternoon and found the Russian Section.

"OK, Youriko, this is your last chance to pull out and come and live with me in luxury in Canada! What d'you say? Only joking! The look on your face... Come on, let's go in, but let me do all the talking". They entered through the revolving door and approached the receptionist.

"Would you ask the head of the Russian Department if he could spare us two minutes on a personal matter, please?"

She looked them up and down, pressed a button on the phone system and asked.

"Down the corridor, third door on the right. Knock and go right in".

"Thank you. Come on, sis". Chou pointed at the name on the door, tapped it and walked in, holding it open behind her for Youriko.

"Good afternoon, ladies, please take a seat, how may I help you?"

"It's like this, Professor Brown, a dear friend of ours, William Davies, is studying here. We have just come over from Canada and would like to surprise him. He has no idea we're here, you see. We met last year in Leningrad. If he is here today do you think we could pop our heads around the door and arrange to meet him later?"

"Yes, I don't see why not. Wait a moment, please, I'll just locate him".

He rang his secretary and asked where William's class was being held.

"They are just down the corridor in the new language lab, I'll take you there myself".

"Thank you ever so much, Professor Brown, could we ask just one more teensy-weensy favour?"

He led them to the language lab, knocked the door and went in, leaving the women outside. He spoke to the teacher in a whisper, and she spoke into the microphone, which took precedence over the tapes playing in the students' earphones. They removed them and waited.

"Thank you, ladies and gentlemen, Professor Brown has an important announcement to make.

"Thank you, Miss Quinn, I want to introduce you to two new members of staff who have just joined us as exchange teachers, they will be specialising in conversational Russian, the vernacular. I'd like you to give them a warm welcome. Ladies, please step inside.

"Dobrie dyen, tovarishshi, kak vee pezhivayete – Good day, comrades, how are you?" they said smiling.

"Dobree dyen. Khorosho, spasiba, tovarishi... Good day. Well, thanks, comrades..." replied the students.

"It can't be?! Is that you, Youriko?" asked Will.

She ran over to him then the rest of the class recognised her too and applauded.

Chou took Youriko on a shopping spree while Will finished his classes, but they met up later at the hotel. Chou and Will became good friends during the week she stayed with them. The afternoon before she left, she organized it so that she and Youriko were in a bank on the pretext of opening an account for the money that GCHQ had given her. A phone call to Youriko's contact number made that effortless, but they had to use Will's student bedsit address for the bank books and ATM cards to be sent to.

"Put this into that account too, please," she said to the deputy manager who was dealing with them. Youriko saw the look of surprise on his face as he scrutinised the cheque, but she didn't realise why until she saw him write two hundred and fifty thousand Canadian dollars in the deposit box on the form.

"I can't let you give me that much", she said.

"Yes, you can, and you will, sis. I've told you before, I'm loaded because of you and you are my impoverished sister. Honestly, I feel mean only giving you that much. My apartment is worth more than twice that and I own that outright. By the way, you will have to bring that gorgeous man over to Toronto for a holiday next year".

The following summer, Will passed his final exams and obtained a BA Bachelor's Degree with Honours, then they took the rest of the summer off and spent it with Will's parents in South Wales. They loved Youriko and treated her like a daughter, so Will made her a daughter-in-law by marrying her in a Cardiff registry office on her birthday on August the fourteenth. His parents might have preferred a more traditional church wedding, but they understood that she had been raised an atheist with a Muslim background.

Then Will entered the training, which would start him on his diplomatic career, just as Youriko had eight years before. She found it hard to be a diplomat's wife at first, because she was used to playing a more active rôle, but she gradually found that she could help with local charities wherever they were stationed and she taught English to the local staff and their children.

When Yuri Andropov succeeded Leonid Brezhnev in November 1982, she sent him a letter congratulating him on his promotion and she meant it.

If it hadn't been for him, she wouldn't be travelling the world with the only man she had ever loved. She took pleasure in explaining that to people who didn't understand how she could have respect, if not affection, for the man who had put her in the labour camp. Andropov actually replied to her letter with an official invitation to his inaugural ceremony in Moscow, with a handwritten note on the bottom thanking her most sincerely and his signature. It was one of her most treasured possessions. When he died fifteen months later, she raised a glass to him and so did Will.

They travelled the world for thirty-seven years in the Diplomatic Service and even stayed at Ankara for two years, but by then anyone who would have met her had moved on. They never did go back to the Soviet Union, although one year while touring the Black Sea they did make it to Sochi and Matsesta to look up Yorgi and his family in the 'Full Bottle' after the break up of the Soviet Union. Not much had changed, except they looked older and the bar looked shabbier. The war in neighbouring Abkhazia and Georgia had been tough on them and put an end to their international business activities.

Youriko and Will gave a party in the 'Bottle' and asked Yorgi to invite all the people who had been there before and the three men who had helped her escape. It was a very enjoyable evening, but somehow, it was not as joyous a place as it had been. She put it down to the war again. Yorgi and Will got on well and became great buddies for the evening. He asked if Yorgi could take them on the route by which his wife had escaped, but Yorgi refused on the grounds that it was far too dangerous and we wasn't even sure if his friends and their farms existed any longer. There were tears in his eyes as he said it.

Yorgi and Trixy insisted that they stayed at their house instead of a hotel and they were pleased to do so. In the morning, while Trixy and Youriko were cooking breakfast, Youriko gave Trixy a cheque for a thousand pounds. She took it, she had too, but Youriko could see how embarrassed she was. When they left, they promised to go again, but somehow they knew they never would, although they sent and received Happy New Year cards every year, and Youriko phoned every now and again.

They saw Chou almost every year. Either she would fly to them, or they would meet her in Toronto or California, because Youriko was still nervous about being in Toronto after her kidnapping even after the KGB ceased to exist in 1991. Chou preferred to visit them because they moved to a different country every two to four years, so she got to see the capitals of the world at the same time.

She took early retirement when she was fifty-five and eventually sold up and moved to California, as she had been saying she would for thirty years. She bought a beautiful apartment overlooking San Francisco Bay and lived there happily single for the rest of her life. Youriko often wondered why she never married, because she had plenty of admirers, but she put it down to her friend's love of travelling and being her own boss. She had always said that her main reason for wanting to get out of Japan was the stuffy, traditional social rules and she didn't want to have to play the dutiful wife either.

As for Youriko and Will, they enjoyed their stays in Africa the most. Youriko would do all she could for animals and children in distress, but when they retired, it was to southern Spain, Andalucía, where they bought a large plot of land back from the coast near Marbella. They grew oranges and grapes on one section and cared for rescued, abandoned donkeys and mules on the other. However, Youriko never lost her love of horses and riding and bought a pair of beautiful, black Andalusian pure-bred Spanish horses, one for each of them since she had taught Will to love horses and ride over the years. She rode the stallion and he the somewhat quieter mare.

As time passed, they had to have more and more help to run the farm, but they never lost interest in it, and could rarely tear themselves away from there long enough to go away for more than a weekend break. Even after helping out at all became too much, they still liked to sit and watch, and they never stopped funding the rescue centre.

Youriko's health deteriorated rapidly after she passed seventy-five. The doctor, Rhys Jones, a family friend, thought that that could have been the long-term effect of deprivation and when she started to go, so did Will, although he was seven years younger.

They remained on the farm, sitting under the orange trees when they were in bloom or fruit, watching the donkeys or sitting on the hill looking out over the Marina in Marbella, talking about the wonderful life they had had together, until one day Youriko passed away peacefully in her sleep next to Will in their own bed.

After that, Doctor Jones said that he seemed to just lose the will to live and he was correct in his diagnosis.

∞

It was then, dear reader, that I signed myself into this wonderful sanatorium to be looked after by my friend, Dr. Rhys Jones and now that I have told you my darling wife's story, I will be pleased to join her whenever God allows.

I pray that it is soon, because I miss the greatest woman I have ever known more than I will life on Earth without her... Ah, there you are, my dearest Youriko...

Andropov's Cuckoo

21 EPILOGUE

My name is Dr. Rhys Jones. I have been William Davies' physician for the last ten years both before and after he arrived at the sanatorium where he has been staying and where I work. My wife, also a medical doctor, attended William's wife, Youriko, until she died nearly two and a half years ago. The reason that I am writing this epilogue and not William himself is because he passed away peacefully in his sleep one night a month ago. I found him that morning lying as if resting in his bed with a smile on his face and the Dictaphone, that had become his constant companion for the month or so previously, in his hand.

I knew that he had been dictating a book, everyone did, you could say that it has been his driving force in those last few weeks, perhaps he would have died earlier if he had not felt so compelled to finish it. You could say that it gave him a new lease on life. He wrote it, or I should say dictated it, with passion, often with tears streaming down his cheeks. I will admit that sometimes I scolded him because I was afraid that the depth of emotion that he was obviously experiencing might cause another heart attack, but he rarely listened to me.

"Just give me a pill to calm me down, but I have to get on with this", he'd say and I would acquiesce and give him a mild sedative.

I'm pretty certain that he knew the end was near and he wanted to finish the book even if it was the last thing that he ever did, as he often said. He was right on that score too, it looks as if it was.

Anyway, he made me promise, as his closest friend (I will happily admit that it made me feel so very proud when he said that) to get Youriko's story published 'by hook or by crook' as he put it, and that is what I have done, you have just been reading the result.

I knew Will and Youriko for a decade, as I said before, but I had no idea what she had been through before I listened to Will's tapes. It is absolutely stunning that someone can have been through so much and not felt the need to talk about it or complain about it. Will had said that she had spent two years in a forced labour camp, but neither of them said any more than that, and I think he only mentioned it because he thought it might have some bearing on her condition.

You think you know someone and then you realise that you don't know the half of it.

Anyway, I hope that it is not out of place to say this here, but goodbye for now, Will and Youriko, my friends, I know that you are together again where you belong. One day my wife and I will see you again.

RJ

22 AFTERWORD

I, the author of this work, was studying Russian in Leningrad in 1973, when I met an Asian lady and her friends. Her name was Youriko and we became instant friends exactly as I describe it in the book. Everything in the chapters concerning that year in Leningrad is true: the Bibles, the letter from Viktor Feinberg, and the meeting with his son and the imposter.

There were other things too, which I did not put in this story; like the girl who took me home to meet her father. He gave me two icons, which he had 'liberated' from a church as the Red Army chased the Germans out of the country. He had been told to burn any and all religious artefacts, but he had rescued these two and he wanted them to go to a 'good home'. Smuggling them out was scary, and I still have them.

When my term of study was over that year, I returned to Portsmouth University and told people Youriko's story, exactly as it is in this book. However, my girlfriend heard about it and one morning I awoke to the smell of burning paper. My girlfriend had set fire to Youriko's pictures, address etc in the kitchen sink.

Therefore, I never saw her again, but I had told Youriko that I would be back the next summer for another term in Russia. What I did not know was that we would be in Kalinin, not Leningrad. I did not see her that second year, or ever again, but the barman in the Evropayskaya Hotel in Leningrad did tell me that a Soviet woman had phoned several times asking for a man with my name.

Everything up to Youriko seeing me off is true, if I was there, or what she told me if I wasn't. Therefore, her looking for me in the second year is dramatised; her move to the Crimea and her escape to the West are just wishful thinking.

I think about Youriko every week of my life and have done since I was nineteen years old. Youriko would be seventy-one now, if she is still alive.

I have been wanting to write Youriko's story for forty-odd years, so I hope that you enjoyed it.

Regards,

Owen

The End

Bonus chapter of a new book:

DEAD CENTRE

Not Every Suicide Bomber Is Religious!

by

Owen Jones

1 SCHEHERAZADE'S BAGHDAD

Tony was terrified, but he knew that it was his only option. He also knew that in a few minutes' time, there would be hundreds far more terrified than he was right now.

He had his schedule and it was memorised to the second. He could even see the big clock on the wall that he had to work to. He watched the seconds tick down and took deep breaths to calm himself, it was not a particularly hot day, but he was perspiring profusely, so he took his handkerchief from his inside jacket pocket and stopped at a mirror to dab at his face.

He was beginning to calm down, the Valium was working. He had not thought that it would be this easy. He had a hundred metres further to walk and fifteen minutes to do it in. He dawdled, looking at the clothes along the way, and wondered, none of it would matter soon, and he wondered whether it ever should have. Shirts, trousers, suits, men's perfumery... he touched some of them, as you might a flower, then up the escalator to ladies' wear and along the aisles heading for the jewellery department. He knew the way; he had walked the route dozens of times.

Two minutes to go and he felt his heart pick up speed. Wait a few more seconds, don't get to close to the display cabinets, he had been told. In fact, he had been given a line not to cross, and lo and behold, there it was a metre before him. He stood on his mark, the point where two sections of the aisle carpet joined, and pretended to be reading an advertisement

Fifteen seconds to go. He looked around himself, a deep sadness in his eyes.

Ten seconds, he caught a sales assistant's eye and she started to walk towards him, he tried to will her away.

Five seconds, she was speaking to him, but he was not listening.

Four, three, two, one...

Zero.

Boom.

She never heard him say sorry, but then neither she nor Tony existed in this world any longer.

After the deafening explosion, there was complete silence for several seconds and then the screaming started. People were screaming, crying and running for their lives, those who were still able to anyway. There were people and bits of people lying all around and smoke from several fires.

Smoke and cries of agony and smells of fear and Semtex and spatters of Tony and the nice female sales assistant all over the ceiling and clothes and shoppers. The department store's alarm started and so did the sprinkler system seconds later.

Men in black raced in from the emergency staircase, but they were there to help themselves, not the wounded, and they carried machine guns, not medical bags, not that there was any resistance.

∞

The next day, the newspapers reported that at least thirty people had been killed and one hundred and fifty injured in the suicide bombing of a large department store in the centre of Baghdad.

Nothing more was to be read in the papers or to be seen on television, but the insurance world was abuzz about the jewellery heist from the store and so were the world's main intelligence agencies.

Ten and a half million dollars worth of goods had been stolen in the confusion and there were no clues as to the perpetrators. They had Tony on CCTV, but he was also dead. They saw that happen too, but then the camera stopped working. They put the losses down to 'looters, who probably included the security staff and the clean-up personnel' and left it at that.

It was not unheard of for security and clean-up staff to steal items of value that they found while in the process of carrying out their grizzly work. It was a perk and nobody really minded if the wealthy Western insurance companies were defrauded anyway, and if there was a clause against acts of war and terrorism, then some other rich people would foot the bill and that didn't matter to a bobby on the beat either.

Sympathy was reserved wholly for the dead, the maimed and their relatives, not the store owners.

The two most noticeable things about the suicide bombing of Scheherazade's department store were the misery that it caused to mostly local people and the overtime it gave them cleaning the place up, making it safe again and reopening it.

The damage it had caused to the shoppers and staff had been horrific, but the actual damage to the building itself had been negligible, because the walls around the jewellery department had recently been clad with slabs of marble and they had stood up well to the blast from the bomb, which had been designed to kill and to maim, but not to cause structural damage.

The six-millimetre-diameter shot that had surrounded the explosives had been heavy enough to wreck people and display cabinets of toughened glass, but not bring down walls or ceilings. However, not many people were aware of that, and neither had Tony been.

The inquiry into the blast began immediately that afternoon when the store's security staff handed their cameras' recordings to the police so that they could start trying to track down those responsible.

The surveillance cameras were mounted on very obvious 'glitter globes', six on each, hanging from the ceilings at such points around the store that every aspect was covered by a camera. Not all of the cameras were recording all of the time, but each one came 'on' for ten seconds before focus was switched to the next camera lens. The globes had been installed and the switching so set up, that almost every location in the store was under observation all of the time, albeit from different angles and from different focal points.

The Federal Police officers ran the recording sequence back from the detonation, so that they had an image of the bomber and then searched for his entry into the store. When they had found him entering the store, it was easy enough to track his movements. Every officer agreed that, in hindsight, it was easy to see that he had something to hide by his demeanour, if not by his clothing. He certainly had not looked 'padded out'.

Six officers watched the footage on both a large screen and a smaller one, because the large screen produced a pixellated image, although individual frames could be corrected to a large extent by software made for the purpose.

They watched Tony, although they did not know his name, for the almost twenty minutes he was in the department store at normal speed and then they watched the footage in slow motion.

Several times.

They watched, and spent all night watching, the film, over and over again, while scenes of crime forensic experts and other police and army officers inspected the gruesome aftermath.

At daybreak, fourteen hours later, they had to stop, and reluctantly went home for some rest. The night shift took over, but on overtime until the day shift could get back in five hours later. They watched the footage over and over again and made notes, which they could share with their colleagues.

One point that everyone on both shifts agreed on, was that it was obvious that the bomber was nervous and the chief officer of the night shift wrote a memorandum to include parts of the film in a training video for store security staff on how to spot people acting suspiciously. However, for the rest they were stumped.

When the day shift took over again, they sat with a coffee and played the film again in slow motion.

"Sir, stop it there! Rewind it a few seconds, please, now, one frame at a time and get ready to freeze it when I say so," said a young female Federal Police officer. "I think I saw something... See there? The perp just mopped his brow, and look! There is brown on his handkerchief! It was either very dusty yesterday, or... I think our man is wearing make-up, stage make-up. We, or I at least, have assumed that he is from the Middle East, but now I am not sure. Look, his forehead is a little whiter now... patchy. Go back and play that sequence again, sir, if you please. See what I mean?

"Could he be European?"

They ran and re-ran that part of the footage over and over again.

"Suzette, you might just have something there," said the commanding officer, Federal Police Captain Ali Allawi, what do you guys think?"

Most agreed, some reluctantly.

"So, our bomber might not be Arab or even from these parts at all. I did notice that he did not shout 'Allahu Akbar!' at detonation."

"Can you give us a clear close-up of his face?"

The female IT expert twiddled some knobs and moved a few virtual sliders in order to enhance the image until it was the best she could produce.

"Sir."

"Throw it up on both screens and print off a dozen hi-res copies, please."

The officers inspected the screens and the print-outs in minute detail.

"Can you manipulate this image, Lieutenant? Try removing those heavy eyebrows... and the moustache, and lighten his skin, especially around the eyes. That's it, a bit paler, north European. Yes...

"Good. Now give him brown hair instead of black, yes, that's it. He could be European or of European descent, but it's only a long shot... a very long shot... Has Scenes of Crime found any bits of him that we could use for ID?"

"No, sir, not yet. Not that I am aware of. The blast took out the nearest pod of cameras and the flash from the explosion over-exposed images from other cameras near-by, so we don't know where any of him flew off to, sir."

"OK, give someone at forensics a call and check."

"Sir! Will do right away, sir! When I called fifteen minutes ago they said that there is massive carnage and anything could belong to anyone within twenty metres of the bomber. They said that it is hard to impossible to check for any DNA matches on the walls and the ceiling because of smoke damage. Pollution, sir."

"All right, lieutenant. Keep in touch with them and let me know the minute anything happens – day or night, on shift or not, understand?"

"Yes, sir."

"OK, guys, for the rest of this shift, we will work on the assumption that the bomber was a white European or American. I will put that in our shift log, but for the time being, it is only speculation, all right? It does not, and I repeat most strongly, it definitely does not, rule out the possibility that he was an Arab terrorist, who committed this atrocity for political or religious motives.

"Who knows what is running through the mind of someone who is on the verge of meeting Allah and taking innocent people with him? Perhaps he just forgot to say 'Allahu Akbar'. Perhaps he hadn't seen the need to wash his face that morning, in the circumstances... Do not allow your minds to close off any possibility. I am only saying that for the rest of this shift, we will run with Suzette's idea that he might be European, or American, let's say Caucasian, and see where it takes us. There is absolutely no historical evidence relating to Caucasian suicide bombers.

"White people bomb things, yes, and blow other people up, yes, but they don't normally kill themselves in the process, at least, not on purpose.

"Our man here is on a mission and he is going to die. If he is Caucasian, then we are dealing with a new breed of suicide bomber, a type no-one has ever met before.

"Question. How many Caucasians were at the scene of the crime at the time of the blast? Someone find out.

"Let's see how many unclaimed teeth we can find, and bits of bone. Get them all off for DNA testing. Let's see whether we have any unattributable body parts of Caucasian origin."

"Forensics are not going to be happy about that, sir. It'll take them weeks, if not months."

Who cares what they think. It can't be helped, we could be on the brink of something new here. A new terrorist organisation or a new splinter group, although I must say that if that is true, why would a Caucasian blow himself up in an Iraqi department store?

"It doesn't make sense! Christians just don't do that sort of thing simply to prove a point.

"Has any group claimed responsibility yet?"

"No, sir, nothing at all from any of the usual sources."

"Have you phoned our sources and asked them?"

"That is being done as we speak, sir, and individual officers are asking their snouts too, but nothing whatsoever… leastwise, not yet."

∞

The men in black ransacked the jewellery display cabinets, most of which had been damaged in the blast and would not resist even a kick, others were machine gunned. The eight combatants took everything they could find in the eight minutes that they had allowed themselves.

A guard on the stairs landing dropped flash grenades down the stairwell at irregular intervals to deter people from coming up or down and the lifts and escalators were disabled.

They had not had to hurt any more people, but they were prepared to do so, if it were necessary. Since they were only on the second floor, it was not a problem to shoot out one of the large windows and abseil down into the two large open-topped, high-sided trucks that were waiting in the alley below.

The trucks left in opposing directions, so that there was less chance of them both being apprehended. However, they were heavily armed and there were rocket launchers waiting in each vehicle. They got away safely without incident and transferred to nondescript commercial vans with souped-up engines shortly after leaving Scheherazade's.

All of the attackers, except Tony, were safely in their hide-out – their boss' villa – within an hour of the atrocity.

"So, Mustapha, everything went according to plan?"

"Yes, sir. We have the merchandise and without conflict of any kind or loss of life on our part.

"Your plan worked totally effectively, sir."

"Yes, it was foolproof because it was simple. I watched everything up to the point of the explosion from the subject's camera on that monitor and then I watched your operation from the footage relayed by your helmet camera too. I saw the whole thing. More than you did. The footage from your camera was a bit patchy though, perhaps because of the speed you were operating at, I suppose."

Mustapha did not want to contradict his powerful boss, so just let it ride.

"Probably, sir," he said, thinking that that was the least likely cause of the interference, but not knowing for certain what it could have been, unless it was due to the electrical shorting of the overhead surveillance cameras, as he suspected.

"You and your team have done well, Mustapha and I shall not forget it. Please convey my pleasure to your squad and be assured that I have given orders for the usual celebrations after a successful mission. You have all deserved it."

"Thank you, sir, I shall tell the men."

"That is all for now, Mustapha, get some rest and then enjoy life."

"Yes, sir," Mustapha saluted his boss and left the room.

When he had left, 'The Boss' picked up his cell phone and typed in a series of numbers.

"Our team won! Let's hope that they win the league as well."

"Good, that is my desire also. When is the next game?"

"I am not certain of the fixture yet, but I think in a few weeks, but it will be an away game… perhaps in your vicinity. Will you be able to put us up if we go?"

"Yes, I think I can arrange that. Just send me the details of when and how many will arrive and it will be taken care of."

"Good. Then I can assume that you will pass on the good news to our friends?"

"Oh, certainly! Everyone likes to be the bearer of good tidings. I hope to see you soon."

"You will, I am sure and I hope the same. Goodbye for now."

∞

"Hello, yes. Are you happy with the results, sir?"

"Yes, everything went perfectly, according to plan. I am most happy with your service."

"Good, I am happy to hear it. So, I can expect you to fulfil your obligation soon?"

"Yes, it has already been arranged. Your company should receive delivery from mine within thirty minutes. If it does not, please do not hesitate to contact me within the hour and I will sort it out immediately.

"Will the service be available again?"

"Yes, of course."

"At the same notice?"

"I cannot guarantee anything without more details from you and completion of this contract, naturally."

"Yes, of course, I understand. Well, I am more that satisfied with your services. Everything has been arranged, so please expect another order from us soon."

"As you say, so shall it be done. I am glad that you have had satisfaction from our company."

Then the line went dead and he got onto his secretary immediately to ensure that the payment from Switzerland was indeed being made.

He did not want any cock-ups with this supplier.

∞

A Swiss bank silently moved $1,500,000 one way and $500,000 in another.

∞

"That was another successful operation, Bob."

"Yes, sir, so it seems."

"There is no need to still call me 'sir', Bob, those days are long gone and I have asked you to call me Gareg numerous times."

"Yes, sir, you have. Sorry, but old habits die hard. Sorry, sir, Gareg."

"Jesus, Bob, 'Sir Gareg' is even worse!" he said jokingly.

"Yes, er, Gareg, I'll get used to it one day, I suppose."

"I hope so. Try to relax a bit more, we're not in the army any longer and haven't been for ages. Five for you and ten for me, I think, or not?"

"Yes, s… er, Gareg. I left four years ago and will always be grateful that you looked me up and took me on. I was so worried that I'd end up on the scrapheap, like so many old soldiers."

"Yes, well, I wasn't going to let that happen, after all we've been through together, was I?"

"Well, sir, I mean, er, Gareg, you have turned my life around and there is no mistake about that. Me and the missus were worried about what I would do when I retired from the forces, but here I am earning three times more with you than before, and I've still got my pension. I just wish that poor old Jenny was here to see the benefit. Still, I am indebted to you and always will be."

"Enough of all that now, let's open a bottle of scotch to another mission well done or would you rather go into town and sink a few pints?"

"Up to you, sir, either way suits me."

"OK, let's have a change and go into town. See who's about. We can always come back if it's quiet."

"Right you are, I'll bring the car around. The Merc or the Bentley?"

"Oh, I think the Bentley tonight. If we drink too much, you know how much it impresses the police. We may even get lucky, you never know."

As they left the farm in high spirits, a doctor from Birmingham, Alabama, was trying to get through, but they were on a mission again and didn't care.

They never did. In their line of business there was no competition and customers always got back to them, because the rate of return on investment was as high as people's ideas.

∞

The money that had changed hands filtered down as did the compensation for the victims of the blast and the overtime money for the police, builders and hospital staff.

Although there were a lot of people grieving, there was also a large injection of capital into the micro-economies of several local communities both in the Scheherazade department store area and other places around the world.

There were no really poor people killed in the blast, although a lot of the sales assistants were related to poor families, and all the wealthy shoppers, and the workers were insured, as was the owner.

Many people made a lot of money from the atrocity, and insurance premiums were flagged to rise the following year to compensate, but that was never made public either.

Andropov's Cuckoo

About the Author

Owen Jones was born in Barry, South Wales, where he lived until going to Portsmouth to study Russian at 18. After finishing his degree, he moved to s'Hertogenbosch in the Netherlands where he lived for ten years.

At 32, Owen moved back to Barry to work with in his family's construction company, first as a painter and then as a director, or, as the bank once corrected him, a painter and decorator. He was also office manager for ten years.

At the age of 50 Owen moved to Thailand to live with a Thai girl that he had met while there on holiday. He married the woman and now lives in her village of birth in remote northern Thailand.

As Owen puts it:

'Born in the Land of Song,

Living in the Land of Smiles'.

Andropov's Cuckoo

Review

Would you, please, leave a review of this book at the address where you bought it right now, please, before you forget

It will help the author and the readers, who come after you... it really will. Your opinion counts more than you may think it does.

Thank you,

Owen

PS: Please be my friend and keep in touch using the following contact details:

BlueSky: owen-author.bsky.social
https://tiktok.com/@owen_author
http://twitter.com/owen_author
https://facebook.com/angunjones
http://meganpublishingservices.com
http://owencerijones.com

Andropov's Cuckoo

Owen Jones

Books by the Same Author

Alien House
A Story of Love, Hope and Alien Intervention

-

Andropov's Cuckoo
A Story of Love Intrigue and The KGB

-

Annwn – Heaven - *series*
A Night in Annwn
The Strange Story of Old Willy Jones's NDE
Life in Annwn
The Story of Willy Jones's Life in Heaven
Leaving Annwn
Returning to Earth on a Mission!

-

Asian Shorts
An Anthology of Short Stories Involving Asians or Asia

-

Behind The Smile - *series*
The Story of Lek, a Bar Girl in Pattaya
Volume I: **Daddy's Hobby**
Volume II: **An Exciting Future**
Volume III: **Maya – Illusion**
Volume IV: **The Lady in the Tree**
Volume V: **Stepping Stones**
Volume VI: **The Dream**
Volume VII: **The Beginning**

-

Daisy's Chain
A Story of Love, Intrigue and the Underworld on the Costa del Sol

-

Dead Centre - series
Dead Centre
Not All Suicide Bombers Are Religious!
Dead Centre II
Even The Wrong Can Be Right Sometimes!

-

The Bull at the Gate
The Day the Sky Fell!

-

The Disallowed
The Story of a Contemporary Vampire Family

-

Fate Twister
The Strange Story of Wayne Gamm

-

The Bull at the Gate
The Day the Sky Fell!

-

The Ghouls of Calle Goya
When Malice Results From Good Intentions!

-

The Psychic Megan Series
A Spirit Guide, A Ghost Tiger, and One Scary Mother!

The Misconception
Megan's Thirteenth
Megan's School Trip
Megan's School Exams
Megan's Followers
Megan and the Lost Cat
Megan and the Mayoress
Megan Faces Derision

Owen Jones

Megan's Grandparents' Visit
Megan's Father Falls Ill
Megan Goes on Holiday
Megan and the Burglar
Megan and the Cyclist
Megan and the Old Lady
Megan's Garden
Megan Goes to the Zoo
Megan Goes Hiking
Megan and the W. I. Cooking Competition
Megan Goes Riding
Megan and the Radio One Beach Party
Megan Goes Yachting
Megan at Carnival
Megan's Christmas
Megan Catches Covid-19

-

Tiger Lily of Bangkok – *Series*
Volume I: **Tiger Lily of Bangkok**
When the Seeds of Revenge Blossom!
Volume II: **Tiger Lily of Bangkok in London**
The Tiger Re-awakens!

-

Non-Fiction

How to Give Your Dog a Real Dog's Life
(and make him love you for it)

-

The Eternal Plan
– *Revealed*
(written by Colin Jones, compiled by Owen Jones)

-

Authorship
Publishing Your Book On You Own

Andropov's Cuckoo

Plus 195 other self-help manuals.

www.ingramcontent.com/pod-product-compliance
Lightning Source LLC
Chambersburg PA
CBHW070545010526
44118CB00012B/1223